Mindfulness with Breathing

# Mindfulness
## with Breathing
*A Manual for Serious Beginners*

Buddhadāsa Bhikkhu

*Translated from the Thai by
Santikaro Bhikkhu*

*Foreword by Larry Rosenberg*

Wisdom

Wisdom Publications
199 Elm Street
Somerville, MA 02144 USA
wisdomexperience.org

First published in 1988
Revised edition published by Wisdom Publications in 1997

*Library of Congress Cataloging-in-Publication Data*
Phra Thepwisutthimethī (Ngūram), 1906–1993
    Mindfulness with breathing : a manual for serious beginners / Buddhadāsa Bhikkhu ; translated from the Thai by Santikaro Bhikkhu.
        p.    cm.
    ISBN 0-86171-111-4 (alk. paper)
        1. Meditation—Buddhism.    2. Ānāpānasmṛti.    3. Tipiṭaka. Suttapiṭaka. Majjhimanikāya. Ānāpānasatisutta—Criticism, interpretation, etc.    I. Santikaro, Bhikkhu, 1957–    .
        II. Tipiṭaka. Suttapiṭaka. Majjhimanikāya. Ānāpānasatisutta. English. III. Title.
    BQ5612.P53    1996
    294.3'443—dc20                                                                                96–32332
    0 86171 111 4

ISBN 978-0-86171-111-6      ebook ISBN 978-0-86171-716-3
25  24  23  22
12  11  10  9

Cover design by TLrggms. Interior design by: LJ.Sawlit
Cover photo by Gregory Palmer / kinworks.net

Wisdom Publications' books are printed on acid-free paper and meet the guidelines for permanence and durability of the Committee on Production Guidelines for Book Longevity of the Council on Library Resources.

Printed in the United States of America.

MIX
Paper from
responsible sources
FSC® C011935

Visit fscus.org.

# Contents

# Anumodanā

*To all Dhamma comrades, those helping to spread Dhamma:*

Break out the funds to spread Dhamma to let faithful trust flow,
  Broadcast majestic Dhamma to radiate long living joy.
Release unexcelled Dhamma to tap the spring of virtue,
  Let safely peaceful delight flow like a cool mountain stream.
Dhamma leaves of many years sprouting anew, reaching out,
  To unfold and bloom in the Dhamma centers of all towns.
To spread lustrous Dhamma and in hearts glorified plant it,
  Before long, weeds of sorrow, pain, and affliction will flee.
As virtue revives and resounds throughout Thai society,
  All hearts feel certain love toward those born, aging, and dying.
Congratulations and blessings to all Dhamma comrades,
  You who share Dhamma to widen the people's prosperous joy.
Heartiest appreciation from Buddhadāsa Indapañño,
  Buddhist science ever shines beams of Bodhi long lasting.
In grateful service, fruits of merit and wholesome successes,
  Are all devoted in honor to Lord Father Buddha.
Thus may the Thai people be renowned for their virtue,
  May perfect success through Buddhist science awaken their hearts.
May the King and his family live long in triumphant strength,
  May joy long endure throughout this our world upon earth.

*Buddhadāsa*

*Mokkhabalārāma*
*Chaiya, 2 November 2530 (1987)*
*Translated by Santikaro Bhikkhu*
*3 February 2531 (1988)*

# Foreword

IN HAPPILY ACCEPTING the invitation to write about Ajahn Buddhadāsa's teaching of *ānāpānasati* I have come full circle from an encounter I had with him in Thailand a number of years ago. At that time, I had already corrected the misconception I had previously held, one which is shared by many practitioners, that *ānāpānasati* is simply a method to calm the mind, that it is solely *samatha*. According to this view, you calm the mind by paying continuous and exclusive attention to the breath until the mind is serene and fit to do some serious "looking." At this point, this view asserts, you can drop the breath and get on with the "real work" of *vipassanā*. However, I knew this was not so. The breath awareness teaching in the *Ānāpānasati Sutta* provides a clear and comprehensive way for us to develop *both samatha* and *vipassanā*. The Buddha himself is reported to have attained liberation using this very method. Before I met Ajahn Buddhadāsa, however, my understanding of this was largely conceptual.

This all changed during an intense two-hour meeting with Ajahn Buddhadāsa at his monastery, Suan Mokkh, in southern Thailand. The impact of this encounter changed my practice and teaching forever. Buddhadāsa was nearly eighty when I saw him, and though his health was not very good, he was still tireless in his teaching. He often taught informally, sitting in front of his hut in the forest with students—and wild chickens and a dog!—gathered around him. From time to time bus loads of people seeking his blessing would come to Suan Mokkh. He would patiently and lovingly care for these visitors and then resume our conversation at exactly the same point at which we had paused.

He was convinced that the *Ānāpānasati Sutta* provided a magnificent vehicle for practice and teaching. With detailed, painstaking, and quietly passionate instructions, he took me through the sixteen contemplations of the sutta step by step, contemplation by contemplation. It was a mixture of lecture and meditative reflection, and one of the most powerful pieces of teaching I have ever experienced.

His approach was rational and systematic, but also beautifully timed to open me up emotionally. Its effect was dramatic. As you will soon discover, the sutta is comprised of four tetrads, or four sets of four contemplations. Briefly, in the first tetrad we familiarize ourselves with the breath and the body; in the second, breathing with feelings; in the third, breathing with mental formations; and in the fourth set of contemplations we concern ourselves with the breath and discernment—pure *vipassanā*. This last set of contemplations, 13–16, is about impermanence, emptiness, and letting go into the freedom that emerges naturally from such clear seeing.

When Ajahn Buddhadāsa and I had completed the thirteenth contemplation he paused, seemingly to check if I had understood thus far. When he was convinced that I did, he quickly and decisively said, "Okay, now you can go back to contemplations 1–12, with which by now you are quite familiar. You will find that the object of each and every one of these contemplations is impermanent and empty: the body is empty; feelings are empty; mental formations are empty; and the in- and out-breaths, which have accompanied you throughout the contemplations, are also empty. Of course breathing is happening, but you will see that no matter how hard you look, there is no 'breather' to be found anywhere!" His warm, large smile and laughter ended the interview.

In this book, Ajahn Buddhadāsa will take you by the hand and lead you, as he did for me, all the way from the first attempt to observe the in- and out-breaths to the kinds of insight that have the power to liberate. Of course, you will begin with merely a set of instructions, but then you must take these clear words of teaching and put them into practice. If you do, you will not be disappointed. The beauty of this work is its seamless integration of theory and practice. You have in your hands a precious yogic manual, one that can decisively launch you into the practice of *vipassanā* meditation and set you firmly on the Buddha's path of liberation.

I bring both of my palms together in the heartfelt wish that these simple, clear teachings of Ajahn Buddhadāsa bring as much benefit into your life as they have already brought into mine. I bring both palms together with gratitude to this great servant of the Buddha.

*Larry Rosenberg*
*Cambridge Insight Meditation Center*

# Preface to the Revised Edition

THE MAIN BODY of this manual comes from the series of lectures given during Suan Mokkh's September 1986 meditation course. For this course, Ajahn Poh (Venerable Bodhi Buddhadhammo, the initiator of these courses and currently Suan Mokkh's Abbot) asked Ajahn Buddhadāsa to give the meditation instruction to the retreatants directly: usually they are given by other monks, such as the translator. Each morning, after breakfast, the retreatants gathered at "the Curved Rock," Suan Mokkh's outdoor lecture area. Venerable Ajahn spoke in Thai, with this translator interpreting into English. The talks were recorded and many people, both foreign and Thai, requested copies of the series.

At the request of the Dhamma Study-Practice Group, the tapes were transcribed and edited for publication. The text follows the original Thai closely, although some of the translator's interpolations have been kept. Material from talks given during subsequent retreats was added as appendixes to make the manual more comprehensive. In this edition, however, the appendixes have been incorporated into the text. We also include a "Translator's Conclusion" based on a talk given by the interpreter as a summary of the Venerable Ajahn's seven lectures. The final word comes from our prime inspiration and original source: the Lord Buddha's "Mindfulness with Breathing Discourse" (*Ānāpānasati Sutta*). The complete text of this fundamental sutta is presented here in a new translation. We hope that the exquisite simplicity and directness of the Blessed One's words will gather all of the preceding explanations into one clear focus. That focus, of course, must aim at the only real purpose there is in life— *nibbāna*.

This revised edition has been prepared with the help of Wisdom Publications. The material is substantially the same as the previous editions; however, the following changes have been made. Material that was previously in appendixes (that which had been taken from talks given in the months after the main series on which this book is based) has been incorporated into the text, thus expanding chapters one and two into three chapters. The translator's introduction and conclusion have been revised, a few terms have been added to the glossary, and the usual attempts to make the book more accessible, readable, and accurate have been tried. We hope the reader approves of the results.

*Santikaro Bhikkhu*
*Suan Atammayatārāma (Dawn Kiam)*
*2538 Rains Retreat (1995)*

# Translator's Introduction

MINDFULNESS WITH BREATHING is a meditation technique anchored in our breathing. It is an exquisite tool for exploring life through subtle awareness and an active investigation of breathing and of life. The breath is life; to stop breathing is to die. The breath is vital, natural, soothing, revealing. It is our constant companion. Wherever we go, at all times, the breath sustains life and provides the opportunity for spiritual development. In practicing mindfulness upon and through breathing, we develop and strengthen our mental abilities and spiritual qualities. We learn to relax the body and calm the mind. As the mind quiets and clears, we investigate how life unfolds as experienced through the mind and body. We discover the fundamental reality of human existence and learn to live our lives in harmony with that reality. And all the while, we are anchored in the breath, nourished and sustained by the breath, soothed and balanced by the breath, sensitive to breathing in and breathing out. This is our practice.

Mindfulness with breathing is the system of meditation, or mental cultivation (*citta-bhāvanā*), often practiced and most often taught by Buddha Gotama. For more than 2,500 years, this practice has been preserved and passed along. It continues to be a vital part of the lives of practicing Buddhists in Asia and around the world. Similar practices are found in other religious traditions as well. In fact, forms of mindfulness with breathing predate the Buddha's appearance. These were perfected by him to encompass his most profound teachings and discoveries. Thus, the comprehensive form of mindfulness with breathing taught by the Buddha leads to the realization of humanity's highest potential—spiritual awakening and liberation. It has other fruits as well, and so offers something of both immediate and long-term value, of both mundane and spiritual benefit to people at all stages of spiritual development.

In the Pali language of the Buddhist scriptures this practice is called *ānāpānasati,* which means "mindfulness with in-breaths and out-breaths." The complete system of practice is described in the Pali texts and further explained in their commentaries. Over the years, an extensive body of literature has developed. The Venerable Ajahn Buddhadāsa has drawn on these sources, especially the Buddha's words, for his own practice. Out of that experience, he has given a wide variety of explanations about how and why to practice mindfulness with breathing. This book contains some of his most cogent talks about this meditation practice.

The talks included here were chosen for two reasons. First, they were given to Westerners who were attending the monthly meditation courses at Suan Mokkh. In speaking to Western meditators, Ajahn Buddhadāsa uses a straightforward, no-frills approach. He does not go into the cultural interests of traditional Thai Buddhists; instead, he prefers a scientific, rational, analytical attitude. And rather than limit the instruction to Buddhists, he emphasizes the universal, natural humanness of *ānāpānasati.* Further, he endeavors to respond to the needs, difficulties, questions, and abilities of beginning Western meditators, especially our guests at Suan Mokkh.

Second, this manual is aimed at "serious beginners." By "beginner" we mean people who are fairly new to this practice and its theory. Some have just begun, while others have some practical experience but lack information about where and how to develop their practice further. Both types of beginners can benefit from an overall perspective and clear instructions concerning their current situation. By "serious" we mean those who have an interest that runs deeper than idle curiosity. A serious individual will read and reread this manual carefully, will think through this information adequately, and will apply the resulting understanding with sincerity and commitment. Although some people like to think that we do not have to read books about meditation, that we need only to do it, we must be careful to know what it is we are doing. In order to practice meaningfully, we must begin with some source of information that is sufficiently clear and complete. If we do not live near a competent teacher, a manual such as this is necessary. The beginner needs information simple enough to give a clear picture of the entire process, yet with enough detail to turn the picture into reality. This manual should strike the proper balance. There is enough to guide successful practice, but not so much as to complicate and overwhelm. Those who are serious will find what they need without difficulty.

If you have yet to sit down and "watch" your breath, this book will point out the benefits of doing so and will explain how to begin. Still, until you try it, and keep trying, it will be impossible to completely understand these words. So read this book through at least once, or as many times as it takes to get the gist of the practice. Then, as you practice, read and reread the sections most relevant to your particular stage. Only through applying them will these words become tangible. When properly put into practice, they will guide your development more securely. This manual should provide you with enough intellectual understanding to be clear about what you need to do and how to go about doing it. As you focus on the immediate requirements of today's learning, do not lose sight of the overall path, structure, method, and goal. Then you will practice with confidence and success.

In addition to its primary purpose—teaching how to practice *ānāpānasati* correctly—this manual serves another purpose that the casual reader might overlook. In the course of carefully studying in the way that has been recommended here, you will discover that every central teaching of Buddhism, true Buddhism in its pristine form, is mentioned here. Thus, this book provides an outline of the essential teachings of Buddhism. So in this way our intellectual study is neatly integrated with our mental cultivation practice. For how can we separate the two? To fully understand our practice we must do our Dhamma homework, and vice versa. Having both in one place will help those who are confused about what and how much to study. Just be sure that you understand all the things discussed here; that is enough.

We should always remember that meditation is the cultivation and practice of non-attachment. The Buddha taught only the middle way, and *ānāpānasati* is nothing but the middle way. It is neither an intense practice, nor can it be done without effort. It must be done with balance. Properly done, *ānāpānasati* is neither detached pushing away nor egoistic clinging; it is a practice of non-attachment. Be very careful about sitting down with ideas like, "I am sitting, I am watching, I am breathing, I am meditating. I am this, that is mine, my breathing, my body, my mind, my feelings, I, I, me, me, mine, mine..." Learn to let go of these attached feelings and ideas of "I" and "mine." Learn to stay balanced in the breathing with *sati*.

We do not cling to the technique we are using, nor do we cling to its theory. We do not use *ānāpānasati* to collect mundane trivia about the breath, ourselves, or anything else. We do not abuse it in the pursuit of attainments. Rather, we respectfully use *ānāpānasati* to develop the skills and learning we need, and all we need is to let go of attachments and thereby quench our *dukkha*.

The middle way is also a practice of correctness, of being skillful in the way we live. While practicing *ānāpānasati* correctly, we are also living correctly. We do no harm to any creature, neither to others nor to ourselves. This practice abuses no one. As we become established in this practice, we become familiar with a mode of being that is correct, balanced, and non-attached. We do not get caught up in extremes, in any of the dualistic traps. Although we may initially develop this wisdom in formal *bhāvanā* practice, we then perfect it within the informal meditation of daily life.

Attachment is a long-established habit for most of us. If we could drop it easily, we would become buddhas just like that! Instead, most of us must work at letting go of our attachments and the habit of clinging and grasping. *Ānāpānasati* is one way of letting go. We begin by letting go of our coarse attachments: attachments to the body, to aches and pains; attachments to agitation and impatience, to boredom and laziness; attachments to external disturbances and petty annoyances. Then, we find ourselves becoming attached to more subtle things, such as happy feelings. Once we let go of these, we discover attachments to higher, brighter, clearer, more refined states of awareness. Letting go of these, we begin to have some insight into reality and so we become attached to the insights. Finally, we learn to let go of everything. In this way, *ānāpānasati* is a systematic method of successively letting go of more and more subtle attachments until there is no attachment left at all.

The benefits of correct, sustained *ānāpānasati* practice are numerous. Some are specifically religious, whereas others are mundane. Although Ajahn Buddhadāsa covers them extensively in the seventh lecture, we should mention a few here at the beginning. First, *ānāpānasati* is good for both our physical and mental health. Long, deep, peaceful breathing is good for the body. Proper breathing calms us and helps us to let go of and eliminate the tension, high blood pressure, nervousness, and ulcers that ruin so many lives these days. We can learn the simple and beautiful act of sitting quietly, alive to our breathing, free of stress, worry, and anxiety. This gentle calm can be maintained in other daily activities and will allow us to do everything with more grace and skill. *Ānāpānasati* brings us into touch with reality and nature. We often live in our heads—in ideas, dreams, memories, plans, words, and the like. So we do not even have the opportunity to understand our own bodies, never taking the time to observe them (except when the excitement of illness or sex occurs). In *ānāpānasati*, through breathing, we become sensitive to our bodies and their nature. We ground ourselves in this basic reality of human existence, which provides the stability we need to cope wisely with feelings, emotions, thoughts, memories, and all the rest of our inner conditioning. No longer blown about by these experiences, we can accept them for what they are and learn the lessons they have to teach us. We begin to learn what is what, what is real and what is not, what is necessary and what is unnecessary, what is conflict and what is peace.

With *ānāpānasati* we learn to live in the present moment, the only place one can truly live. Dwelling in the past—which has died—or dreaming of the future—which brings death—is not really living as a human being ought to live. Each breath, however, is a living reality within the boundless here-now. To be aware of the breath is to live, ready to participate fully in whatever comes next. Lastly, *ānāpānasati* helps us to let go of the selfishness that is destroying our lives and our world. Our societies and planet are tortured by the lack of peace. The problem is so serious that even politicians and military-industrialists pay lip service to it. Still, very little is done to encourage the blossoming of genuine peace. Merely external—and superficial—solutions are tried, while the actual source of conflict is internal, within each of us. Conflict, strife, struggle, and competition, violence and crime, exploitation and dishonesty—these all arise out of our self-centered striving, which is born from selfish thinking. *Ānāpānasati* will guide us to the bottom of this nasty "I-ing" and "my-ing" that spawns selfishness. It is not necessary to shout for peace when we need merely to breathe with wise awareness.

Many people who share our aspiration for peace—peace both for individual hearts and for the world we share—visit Suan Mokkh. We offer this manual to them and to all others who seek Lord Buddha's path of peace and who accept this as the duty and joy of all human beings. We hope that this book will enrich your practice of *ānāpānasati* and your life. May we all realize the purpose for which we were born.

*Santikaro Bhikkhu*

# Acknowledgments

### TO THE FIRST EDITION

DHAMMA PROJECTS give us opportunities to join together in meritorious work and in service of our comrades in birth, aging, illness, and death. A number of friends have given freely of their energy, time, and skills. Although there is no better reward than the contentment and peace that comes with our doing our duty in Dhamma, nevertheless, we would like to acknowledge and bless our friends' contributions.

Those who helped are: Jiaranai Lansuchip, Supis Vajanarat, Pradittha Siripan, Dhammakamo Bhikkhu, Viriyanando Bhikkhu, John Busch, Kris Hoover, Sister Dhammadinnā, Wutichai Taveesaksirphol, Phra Dusadee Metaṅkuro, Dr. Priya Tasanapradit, Amnuey Suwankiri, and the Dhamma Study-Practice Group. The support of certain special friends was invaluable: Ajahn Poh (Bodhi Buddhadhammo), Ajahn Runjuan Indrakamhaeng, and Mrs. Pratum Juanwiwat.

Lastly, Ajahn Buddhadāsa, in line with the Blessed One's purpose, gives us the example and inspiration for a life of Dhamma service, which we humbly try to emulate in ways such as putting together this manual.

*Phra Dusadee Metaṁkuro*
*Suan Mokkhabalārāma*
*Twelfth Lunar Month, 2530 (1987)*

### TO THE REVISED EDITION

The entire text was typed onto disk by Ms. Boonsom, while David Ollson and David Mendels helped check her work. Subsequent checking, proofreading, and correcting were undertaken by the

Sangha of *Dawn Kiam*—Dhammavidu Bhikkhu, Samanera Sucitto, Samanera Santipemo, Matthew Magnus, David Wayte, and the translator—during the Rains Retreat of 1995.

Finally, Wisdom and their capable editors, proofreaders, designers, and others have brought this project to fruition. On behalf of Suan Mokkhabalārāma and the Dhammadana Mulanidhi, we express appreciation, gratitude, and blessings for their efforts.

*Santikaro Bhikkhu*
*Suan Atammayatārāma*

# Textual Notes

AJAHN BUDDHADĀSA felt that committed students of Dhamma should become familiar with and deepen their understanding of important Pali terms. Translations into English often miss some, or much, of the original meaning. (Take as an example the Pali term *dukkha*.) By learning the Pali terms, we can explore the various meanings and connotations that arise in different contexts. In this volume, you will find Pali terms explained and sometimes translated (although not always in the same way) both in the text and in the glossary. The spelling we have used is according to Thai convention.

Pali has both singular and plural inflections, but Thai does not. The Pali-Thai terms herein are used like the English word *sheep*, sometimes with an article and sometimes not. Depending on the context and meaning, you can decide which cases are appropriate: singular, plural, both, or numberless.

Generally, Pali terms are italicized. The proper nouns Buddha, Dhamma, and Sangha are not italicized. Pali and Thai scripts do not use capital letters. In general, we have only capitalized Pali terms when they begin a sentence.

All notes have been added by the translator.

# 1

# Why Practice Dhamma?

## WHY DHAMMA? WHY PRACTICE DHAMMA?

Before we answer these questions, we need to understand the meaning of Dhamma. Then we can discuss the reasons why we must study and practice Dhamma.

## DHAMMA AND THE SECRETS OF LIFE

A simple explanation of Dhamma is "the secret of nature that must be understood in order to develop life for the highest possible benefit."

To develop life to the highest level means to reach a stage of life that is free from all problems and all *dukkha* (unsatisfactoriness, suffering). Such a life is completely free from everything signified by the words *problem* and *dukkha*.

To understand our topic, it is also important to clarify the word *secret*. If we do not know the secret of something, then we are unable to be successful in obtaining the highest results and maximum benefits from it. For example, the exploration of outer space and developments in nuclear power have been possible through understanding the secrets of these things. The same is true of life. In order to develop our lives to the fullest, we must know life's secrets. Life, especially in the context of Dhamma, is a matter of nature (*dhamma-jāti*). This Pali word *dhamma-jāti* may not correspond exactly to the English word *nature*, but the two are close enough. Nature, in this context, means something that exists within itself, by itself, of itself, and as its own law. According to this understanding, nature is not opposed to humanity, as some Westerners believe, but encompasses humanity and all that human beings do and experience. Thus, in order to understand Dhamma, we must understand the secret of the nature of life.

## DHAMMA: FOUR ASPECTS

The Dhamma of life has four aspects:

1. nature itself;
2. the law of nature;
3. the duties that must be performed according to that law of nature; and
4. the fruits or benefits that arise from the performance of that duty.

We should always keep these four interrelated meanings in mind.

Please investigate these truths within yourself, within this body and mind that you imagine to be yourself. Within each of us, various natures are compounded into a body, into a being. And there is the natural law that controls these natures. Further, according to the law of nature, there are the duties that must be performed correctly. Lastly, there are the results of the performance of these duties. If one's duties are performed correctly, the result will be well-being, tranquility, and ease. If they are performed incorrectly, however, the result will be *dukkha*: unsatisfactoriness, anguish, pain, frustration, suffering. Even at the beginning, we should observe carefully and see clearly that we can find all four aspects of Dhamma or nature within each of us. When we have thoroughly investigated the four meanings of nature, we will see that all life is made up of these four aspects. At present, however, we have yet to understand them correctly and completely. We have not truly penetrated the secret of what is called "life." As we have not yet realized the secret of Dhamma, we are unable to practice in a way that obtains the fullest benefit from life. Let us take the time to thoroughly study Dhamma and "the secret of life" so we might take full advantage of them.

### DEVELOPING LIFE BEYOND *DUKKHA*

We must also consider the phrase "developing life." As we begin to practice, we do not know the secret of this either. We lack a clear understanding of the extent to which life can truly be developed. As we do not realize the highest benefits that are available to humanity, we take little interest in the secrets of life that are necessary to reach those highest levels. Our objective, then, is to understand how far life can be developed and to kindle interest in that development.

As beginners, we need only hold to the basic principle that "developing life" means "causing life to progress to the highest level," that is, beyond all problems and *dukkha*, beyond all the possible meanings and gradations of these two terms. For those unfamiliar with the word *dukkha*, we can tentatively translate it as "stress, unsatisfactoriness, conflict, agitation—all the things that disturb life." *Dukkha* is what we are running from all the time. *Dukkha* interferes with a life of calm and ease as well as with spiritual perfection. When life is developed beyond all *dukkha*, it reaches its highest possible level.

Now, some people do not know about their own problems. They do not understand *dukkha*, neither in general terms nor in their own lives. They look at themselves and say, "Oh! I don't have any problems; everything is okay." They accept all their difficulties and sorrow as normal and ordinary. Are we like this? We need to take a serious, detailed look into our own lives to see if there is anything that we can call "a problem." Is there any *dukkha*? Is there anything unsatisfactory or disturbing about life? Such questions are necessary when we choose to study Dhamma. If you have not looked inside, if you are unaware of your problems, if you feel no *dukkha*, then you cannot know why you are on retreat, why you have come to a meditation center, or why you are studying Dhamma. Please, take a good, clear look at your problems and *dukkha* before proceeding any further.

## DEVELOPING LIFE IS OUR DUTY

There are four aspects of developing life. The first is to prevent from arising that which is dangerous to life. The second is to eliminate and destroy that which is dangerous that has already arisen in life. The third is to produce that which is useful and beneficial for life. The fourth is to maintain and preserve such beneficial elements so that they grow further. Again, these four aspects of developing life are: preventing new dangers, eliminating old dangers, creating beneficial elements, and maintaining and increasing the beneficial elements. These comprise what is called "developing life." Developing life is our duty. If such development is to happen, we must realize our true duty.

In order to fulfill our duty, we must have in our possession four very important *dhammas*,[1] four Dhamma tools. These four Dhamma tools are *sati* (mindfulness or reflective awareness), *sampajañña* (wisdom-in-action or ready comprehension), *paññā* (wisdom or spiritual knowledge) and *samādhi* (concentration, mental collectedness, and stability). These four tools will enable us to develop life.

In addition, the practice of *vipassanā*, or mental development, cultivates and trains the mind so that these four Dhamma tools are sufficiently enriched to develop our lives. We need to take an interest in studying the mental development of these four necessary *dhammas*.

## THE KIND OF *ĀNĀPĀNASATI* WE NEED

There are many different systems and techniques of mental development, or *vipassanā*, for training the mind. Nevertheless, of all known techniques, the best is *ānāpānasati-bhāvanā*, the cultivation of mindfulness with breathing. This is the practice that we will discuss in detail throughout this book.

The correct and complete practice of *ānāpānasati-bhāvanā* is to take one truth or reality of nature and then observe, investigate, and scrutinize it in the mind with every inhalation and every exhalation. Thus, mindfulness with breathing allows us to contemplate any important natural truth while breathing in and breathing out.

Such study is of great importance and value. To know the truth of something, we must take that reality and contemplate, analyze, and study it wholeheartedly every time we breathe in and out. The object must be experienced continuously in the mind. Here, "continuously" means "with every in-breath and out-breath." Breathing in, know that object. Breathing out, know that object. Breathing in, understand that object. Breathing out, understand that object. This kind of contemplation is necessary, as well as beneficial, to our development of knowledge. Such study brings about a transformation in the mind-heart, that is to say, on the inside of life.

Actually, the meaning of *ānāpānasati* is quite broad: "to recall anything at all with *sati* while breathing in and breathing out." Imagine that while breathing in and breathing out you are thinking about your home or work; or about your family and friends. This too can be called *ānāpānasati*. However, this kind of thinking is not our purpose here. We need to recollect Dhamma, that is, the natural truths that free the mind from the suffering of *dukkha*. If we sufficiently investigate these truths in the mind, we will be free of all our problems and eliminate *dukkha*. In other words, we must acquire the four Dhamma tools mentioned earlier. This kind of *ānāpānasati* is the most useful.

## FOUR OBJECTS TO CONTEMPLATE

What are the proper, correct, and necessary objects of contemplation every time we breathe in and breathe out? There are four proper objects of contemplation: the secrets of *kāya* (body), the secrets of *vedanā* (feeling), the secrets of *citta* (mind), and the secrets of Dhamma. The secrets of these four objects are to be brought into the mind and studied.

These objects are sufficiently important that you should memorize their Pali names. For your own clear understanding and future reference, please remember: *kāya, vedanā, citta*, and Dhamma. These are the four most important topics. Because these four already exist within us as the sources of all our problems, we must use them far more than any other objects to train and develop the mind. Our lack of understanding and inability to master[2] these four objects ensures that they lead us to suffering. Therefore, it is absolutely necessary that we clearly distinguish and understand these four objects: body, feeling, mind, and Dhamma.

## STAGE ONE: FLESH-BODY AND BREATH-BODY

Now, let us examine these four separately, beginning with *kāya*. The Pali word *kāya* literally means "group" and can be applied to any collection of things. In this case, *kāya* specifically means the groups of elements that are compounded together into a physical flesh-and-blood body. The English word *body* can also mean group; we must simply be careful about which group we mean.

Let's observe for ourselves what makes up our bodies. What are the organs? How many are there? What kinds of elements are present? What parts and components come together to form a body? We should note that there is one very important component which nourishes the rest of this body, namely, the breath. The breath too is called *kāya* in that it is a collection of various elements. We will study the establishment of the flesh-body and its relationship to the breath-body.

The breath-body is very important because it sustains life in the rest of the body. This relationship is crucial to our study. Although we lack the ability to control the general body, or flesh-body, directly, we can master it indirectly by using the breath. If we act in a certain way toward the breath-body, there will also be a specific effect upon the flesh-body. This is why we take the breath as the object of our training. Supervising the breath, to whatever degree, is equivalent to regulating the flesh-body to that same degree. This point will be more clearly understood when we have trained up to that particular stage of *ānāpānasati*.

Beginning our practice with the *kāya* (body), we study the breath in a special way. Every kind of breath is noted and analyzed. Long breaths, short breaths, calm breaths, violent breaths, fast breaths, slow breaths—we learn to know them all. We examine the nature, characteristics, and functions of each kind of breath that arises.

We should observe the influence of the different breaths upon the flesh-body. We need to see clearly the great effect that the breath has on the physical body. We observe both sides of this relationship until it becomes clear that the two, the flesh-body and the breath-body, are interconnected and inseparable. See that the breath-body conditions and affects the flesh-body. This is the first step. We make a special study of the breath and come to know the characteristics of all its different forms. In this way, we gain insight into the conditioning effect it has on the flesh-body. This, in turn, will allow us to master the flesh-body by means of regulating the breath.

The purpose of these beginning steps is to know the secrets of the *kāya*, the body. We know that the breath-body, our breathing, conditions the flesh-body. This important secret helps us to use the breath to gain mastery over the body. We discover that by making the breath calm we can relax the flesh-body. If our breathing is calm, the flesh-body will be likewise. Thus, we can regulate our body indirectly through our breathing. Furthermore, we learn that through calming the breath-body and the flesh-body we can experience happiness, joy, and other benefits.

## STAGE TWO: OUR MASTERS, THE FEELINGS

Once we understand the secrets of the *kāya*, we turn to the secrets of the *vedanā* (feelings). The *vedanā* have the greatest power and influence over human beings; indeed, over all living things. This may come as a surprise to you. Nonetheless, the entire world—animals, humans, all living beings—depends on the *vedanā*. All are under the power of the feelings. At first, this may seem unbelievable, so let's examine it in more detail.

Our entire species is forced by the *vedanā* to do their bidding. When *sukha-vedanā* (pleasant feelings) are present, we try to increase these feelings. Pleasant feelings always pull the mind in a certain direction and condition certain activities. *Dukkha-vedanā* (unpleasant, disagreeable feelings) affect the mind and influence life in the opposite direction; again, the results are habitual responses. The mind struggles with these feelings, turning them into problems that cause *dukkha.*

*Vedanā,* or feelings, have great power over our actions. In fact, the whole world is under the command of these *vedanā.* For example, *taṇhā* (craving) can control the mind. Craving itself is first conditioned by feeling. Thus, the *vedanā* have the strongest and most powerful influence over our entire mind. Thus, it is especially important to understand the secrets of the *vedanā.*

People leave Europe and America to come to Suan Mokkh or go to other retreat centers in search of the conditions for *sukha-vedanā.* This is a fact. Even those people who remain at home work for the sake of nurturing *sukha-vedanā.* We are slaves to *vedanā—sukha-vedanā* in particular—all the time. Clearly, we must understand the *vedanā* in order to keep them under control.

In some Pali texts the *vedanā* are described as "conditioners of the mind" (*citta-sankhāra*). Mind, in this instance, arises from our thoughts, desires, and needs. We cannot endure the influence of the *vedanā.* We are not free within ourselves; we think and act under the power of *vedanā.* Feelings condition the mind and force us to act.

If we master the *vedanā,* we will master the world. This statement may seem peculiar at first. However, we shall be able to regulate the world when we are able to regulate the feelings as needed. Then we shall be able to govern the world as it needs to be governed. These days, nobody is interested in mastering the *vedanā*, and as a consequence, the world exists without any proper supervision. Wars, famines, corruption, pollution, all these crises and problems originate from our failure from the start to master the feelings. If we master the feelings, then we can master the world. It is important that we give this some serious thought.

According to Lord Buddha, the causes of everything in the world are rooted in the *vedanā*. All activities occur because the *vedanā* force us to desire and then to act out those desires. Even the rounds of rebirth within the cycle of *saṃsāra*—the cycles of birth and death, of heaven and hell—are themselves conditioned by the *vedanā*. Everything originates in the feelings. To master the *vedanā* is to master the origin, the source, the birthplace of all things. Thus, it is absolutely necessary to understand these feelings correctly and comprehensively. Then we shall be able to master our feelings, and their secrets will never again deceive us into behaving foolishly.

Once we master the highest and most sublime *vedanā*, we can also master the lower, cruder, more petty *vedanā*. When we learn to control the most difficult feelings, we can control the easy, simple, childish feelings as well. For this reason we should strive to achieve the highest level of *vedanā*; namely, the feelings that are born from *samādhi*. If we can conquer the most pleasant *vedanā*, we can be victorious over all *vedanā*. Should you bother to give it a try? Should you endure any difficulties that might arise? Should you spend your precious time on this practice? Let us consider wisely.

It may seem curious that in striving to realize the highest *vedanā* our aim is to control and eliminate these feelings rather than to enjoy and indulge in them. Some people might think it strange to search for the highest *vedanā* only to master and control them. It is important to understand this point correctly. By eliminating these pleasant feelings we obtain something even better in return. We receive another kind of *vedanā*, a higher order of *vedanā*—one that perhaps should not even be called *vedanā*—something more like *nibbāna* or emancipation. So it is not so unusual or strange that we wish to achieve the best *vedanā* in order to eliminate the pleasant feelings.

There are three main points to learn regarding the *vedanā*. First, we must learn to know the *vedanā* themselves, those things that cause feeling in the mind. Second, we should understand how the *vedanā* condition the *citta*, the mind-heart. The *vedanā* stir up thoughts, memories, words, and actions. We need to know this conditioning of the mind. Third, we must discover that we can master the mind by mastering the *vedanā*, just as we can control the flesh-body by regulating the breath. We master the mind by correctly mastering the feelings that condition it, so that the *vedanā* condition the mind in only the proper way. We do this by regulating those elements that condition the feelings, which is equivalent to regulating the feelings themselves. These are the three important points to understand about the secrets of the *vedanā*.

Since the first and second stages of practice both follow the same principle, it is helpful to compare the two. In the stage regarding the body, we learn what conditions the flesh-body and we study it. We analyze that body-conditioner until we know it in great detail and how it conditions the body. Then, by regulating the body-conditioner, we master the body. In this way we make the body calmer and more peaceful. Likewise, that which conditions the mind is feeling. We calm the mind by controlling the *vedanā* so that they do not condition or stir up the mind; or if they do condition the mind, it is in a desirable way. Thus, the first stage regarding the *kāya* and the second stage regarding the *vedanā* follow the same basic principle and are similar in their method of practice.

## STAGE THREE: THE SUBTLE MIND

First, we practice to know the secrets of the *kāya*. Second, we practice to know the secrets of the *vedanā*. Then, after fully mastering the first and second stages, we practice in order to know the secrets of the *citta*. The mind is the director and leader of life. The mind leads; the body is merely the tool that is led. If life is to follow the correct path, we must understand the *citta* correctly until we are able to master it. This requires a special study, because what we call "mind" is very subtle, complex, and profound. We cannot see it with our eyes; something special is needed to "see" it. Such study is fully within our ability with well-trained *sati*, but we must put forth special effort. Do not lose heart or give up! We are more than capable of studying the *citta* so that we may learn its secrets.

It is not possible to know the *citta* directly: that is, we cannot touch it or make direct contact with it. However, it is possible to know the *citta* through its thoughts. If we know the thoughts, we will know the mind. In the material world, for comparison, we cannot know the phenomenon "electricity" in itself. Instead, we know electricity through its properties: current, voltage, power, and so on. So it is with the *citta*. We cannot directly experience it, but we can experience its properties, the various thoughts. During each day, how many kinds of thoughts arise, how many levels of thoughts come up? We learn to observe these different thoughts; this is how we can know the *citta*.

We begin our study of the *citta* by observing the kinds of thoughts that arise. In what ways are these thoughts improper and in what ways are they correct? Does the mind think along defiled or undefiled lines, good or wicked lines? We observe all the possible types of thought until we can thoroughly understand the *citta*. In this way we gradually come to understand the true nature (*dhamma-jāti*) of the mind.

Because of having already trained the *kāya* and the *vedanā*, we are able at this stage to direct the mind as we require. The mind can be made to think in different ways, or it can be kept still. We can make the mind satisfied, or even dissatisfied, if we choose. The mind can experience different kinds of happiness and joy. It can be stilled, calmed, and concentrated in different ways and to different degrees. Finally, the mind can be liberated. We can direct our mind to let go of things that it loves or hates, or to which it is attached. The mind is liberated from all those objects. These secrets of the mind must be practiced in stage three of *ānāpānasati-bhāvanā*.

We must get to know all the different kinds of *citta*. We are able to make the mind glad and content; we can make it stop and be still. Lastly, we can make the mind let go of its attachments. As the mind lets go of things to which it is attached, things that are attached to the mind let go as well. We let go of it all. As we do this, we become expert and well versed in matters of the mind. This is the third lesson of *ānāpānasati*.

## STAGE FOUR: REALIZING THE SUPREME DHAMMA

Having learned the secrets of the body, the feelings, and the mind, we come to the fourth stage, which concerns Dhamma. As mentioned, Dhamma is nature in all its meanings. In this stage, we take the ultimate truth of all natures as the object of our study. "Studying Dhamma" is to study the truth, the fact, that is, the supreme secret of nature. With this knowledge we can live life in the best way. We need to study the secret of the truth that controls life, the truth of *aniccaā, dukkhaā, anattā, suññatā,* and *tathatā.*

> *Aniccaā:* know that all conditioned things are impermanent and in endless flux.
> *Dukkhaā:* know that all concocted things are inherently unable to satisfy our desires.
> *Anattā:* know that all things are not-self.
> *Suññatā:* know that everything is void of selfhood, of "I" and "mine."
> *Tathatā:* know the thusness, the suchness, of all things.

Together, these are the one ultimate truth. We must observe these until they are fully realized so that the mind will never again lose its way. When the mind understands this truth of all reality, it will not make any errors but will keep itself on the path of correctness.

It may seem curious that all truth—*aniccaā, dukkhaā, anattā, suññatā*—ends up with *tathatā.* It may be surprising that the ultimate truth of everything in the universe comes down to nothing but thusness. In Thai, *tathatā* is translated "just like that." It is more difficult in English: "just such, only thus, thusness." It's hard to believe, isn't it? All truth boils down to the typical, ordinary words, "That's the way things are." When we see thusness, the highest Dhamma, nothing is regarded as good or bad, wrong or right, gain or loss, defeat or victory, merit or sin, happiness or suffering, having or lacking, positive or negative. The highest Dhamma is right here in "merely thus," for thusness is above and beyond all meanings of positive and negative, above all meanings of optimism and pessimism, beyond all dualities. This is the end. The truth to be known in stage four is the secret of nature that says all things are "only thus, just so."

To understand Dhamma sufficiently is the first step, but understanding it is not the end. We now see that as the mind begins to let go, to loosen up its attachments, these attachments dissolve away. We experience this until the point where attachment is extinguished. Once attachment is quenched, the final step is to experience that "the mind is free, everything is free." The Pali texts use the phrase "throwing back." The Buddha said that, at the end, we throw everything back. This means that we have been thieves all our lives by appropriating the things of nature as "I" and "mine." We have been stupid and have suffered for it. Now, we have become wise and are able to give things up. At this last step of practice we realize, "Oh! It isn't mine, it belongs to nature." We throw everything back to nature and never again steal anything.

The last step ends in this unusual way with our not being thieves anymore, with freedom from all influences of attachment. The final step of the development of *ānāpānasati* finishes here. To learn the secret of Dhamma is to know that we should be attached to nothing whatsoever, and then never again to become attached to anything. All is liberated. The case is closed. We are finished.

If we choose to give a name to this last step, we can call it "emancipation" or "salvation." All religions seem to have similar goals and to call these goals by similar names. *Our* understanding of emancipation is the meaning just described—ending attachment and throwing everything back to nature. In Buddhism, emancipation means to be free from every type and form of attachment, so that we may live our lives above the world. Although our bodies are in this world, our minds are beyond it. Thus, all of our problems disappear. This is how to develop life to its full potential, using this four-stage method of practice. There are many more details to consider, but we will leave them for later chapters.

In this chapter, we have given a general outline of this system of practice. With this background it should be easy to practice each step as we come to it. In the following chapters, we will describe the practice of *ānāpānasati* itself.

# 2

# Getting Started

MANY DIFFERENT SYSTEMS, forms, styles, and methods of *samādhi-bhāvanā* (mental cultivation through concentration; meditation) or *vipassanā* (meditation for the sake of insight into impermanence, unsatisfactoriness, and not-self) are taught by various teachers under different names. We will discuss the *samādhi-bhāvanā* specifically introduced and recommended by Lord Buddha himself: *ānāpānasati*. This method appears in both brief references and detailed explanations in the Pali *Tipiṭika*. *Ānāpānasati* is the Buddha's system, "the Buddha's *samādhi-bhāvanā*." This system is not the Burmese or Chinese or Sri Lankan style that some people are clinging to these days. Likewise, it is not the system of "ajahn this," "master that," "guru this," or "teacher that" as others are so caught up in nowadays. Nor is it the style of Suan Mokkh or any other *wat*. Instead, this system is simply the correct way as recommended by the Buddha. He declared this form of *samādhi-bhāvanā* to be the one through which he himself realized the Dhamma of Perfect Awakening. Suan Mokkh practices as well as teaches this system. This book deals with this style in particular of *samādhi-bhāvanā*, or *vipassanā*. We recommend the practice of *ānāpānasati*, which is one system of *vipassanā*, the one used at Suan Mokkh and taught by the Buddha.

*Ānāpānasati* has many forms that are short, easy, and incomplete; we have chosen the form that is complete. Consequently, this sixteen-step form of *ānāpānasati* may seem long and detailed, as is fitting for anything complete. For some people it is too long, too detailed, or simply too much for what they need. This is true—it may be more than is necessary for certain people. But for those who want to study and train thoroughly, it is just right. If we want the technique to be complete, it must include all sixteen steps. This is required by nature. The Buddha never taught anything more than necessary or less than complete. Consequently, this sixteen-step *samādhi-bhāvanā* is neither too much nor too little. If you are patient enough to learn all sixteen steps, you will have the complete system. If you are unable to do all sixteen, there is a condensed version that is adequate for those so inclined. However, if you are interested in completeness, you must have the patience to train and practice *ānāpānasati* in its full form.

## MODE OF LIVING

In order to practice *ānāpānasati* satisfactorily, some general preparations are needed. In other words, we must make some adjustments in our mode of living. Our lifestyle and our *ānāpānasati* practice are interrelated. Thus, we shall discuss the kind of lifestyle that supports Dhamma study and *citta-bhāvanā* practice before going into the details of the practice of *ānāpānasati* itself.

Here, we are discussing the *paccaya*. *Paccaya* is a Pali (and Thai) word whose meaning is similar to the English word *condition*, although it has other connotations as well. The *paccaya* are those things that are absolutely necessary for life; thus, they are sometimes translated as "the necessities, or requisites, of life." The *paccaya* are factors that support the existence of life. These necessities, the foundation of our lives, must be correct if we are to study Dhamma and practice meditation successfully. Thus, it is important to give your attention to this important matter.

Generally, most people only pay attention to the four material or bodily conditions: food, clothing, shelter, and medicine. However, it is equally important that we understand the fifth necessity, the *paccaya* for the mind-heart. The first four conditions are for the body alone. The *paccaya* for the mind is what amuses and coaxes the mind into contentment. We might describe this *paccaya* as "entertainment," since it entertains the mind properly and makes it content in the correct way. Without this condition there would be death— mental death. When the bodily necessities are lacking, the body dies; when the mental necessity is missing, the mind dies. We will get to know both the four physical and the one mental *paccaya*, although we are primarily concerned with the fifth necessity, the *paccaya* that nourishes and sustains the mind. Let's consider in detail these four physical and one mental *paccaya*.

## THE MATERIAL NECESSITIES

Let us start with the first material necessity—food. We should eat food that is food. Do not eat food that is "bait." We should understand the crucial distinction between "food" and "bait." We eat food for the proper nourishment of life. We eat bait for the sake of deliciousness. Bait makes us unwise and causes us to eat foolishly, just like the bait on the hook that snags foolish fish. We must eat the kinds of food that are genuinely beneficial for the body, and we must eat in moderation. "Eating bait" means eating for the sake of deliciousness and fun. It is also usually expensive. We must stop swallowing bait and learn to eat only food that is proper and wholesome. This is especially important while staying in Dhamma centers.

If you are eating bait, you will be constantly hungry all day and night. You will always be sneaking off to eat yet more bait. Eating bait impairs our mental abilities. The mind surrenders to the bait and is not fit for the study and practice of Dhamma. On the other hand, when you eat food, it will be at appropriate times and in moderation. There will be little waste and no danger.

Our second condition is clothing. We should wear clothes that fulfill the real meaning and purpose of clothing: good health, protection against annoyances and discomfort, convenience and simplicity, and expression of culture.

Thus, we should wear clothing that is convenient, simple, and a sign of culture. Please do not wear clothing that destroys the culture of oneself or of others. This leads to inappropriateness in ourselves; it hampers mental tranquility. We should give some thought to the second *paccaya*, clothing.

## INTIMATE WITH NATURE

The third condition is shelter; shelter should be adequate, modest, and not excessive. These days, worldly people live in housing that exceeds their needs, costs a great deal, causes difficulties, and leads to worries. Thus, housing becomes a source of ever-greater selfishness. The most appropriate housing for Dhamma practice is that closest to nature, close enough to be called "in camaraderie with nature." It seems that Europeans and Americans seldom live out in the open, on the ground, or close to nature. They tend to live in beautiful, fancy, expensive places. They seem to need to stay in hotels and do not seem to care for the simple monastery meeting hall.[3]

As a condition of our Dhamma practice, we should try to adapt ourselves to housing that is closer to nature. Living in such a way makes it easier to understand and to practice in harmony with nature. We can learn to be contented and even enjoy such plain and simple living together with nature. This will benefit and support our study and practice.

The Lord Buddha is an excellent example in these matters. The Buddha was born outdoors, was enlightened outdoors, taught sitting outside on the ground, lived outdoors, rested out in the open, and died (*parinibbāna*) outdoors. Clearly his life was intimate with nature. We take his example as our standard and are thus content with a simple, natural mode of living. We believe that the founders of all the great religions practiced plain living as well, although perhaps not as thoroughly as the Buddha, who was born, was enlightened, taught, lived, and died in the open air.

By developing a lifestyle that is intimate with nature, we are making it convenient for nature to speak to us. If we are intelligent listeners, we will hear nature's voice more clearly than if we were far away. Intimacy with nature can become the essence of our mode of living.

In English, the words *moderate* and *sufficient* can be vague, so it is important to understand them in their fuller, Thai meaning, as they have been explained above. We should also be careful about the words *good* and *well,* as in, "good living" and "eating well." We do not care for good living and good eating that have no limits. Instead, we prefer to live and eat correctly. All four material *paccaya* are based on the principles of sufficiency and appropriateness. Do not get carried away with good-good-good such that it becomes excessive and luxurious. That would be neither proper nor decent. Please acknowledge this understanding of the four material necessities.

## THE MIND-HEART *PACCAYA*

The fifth necessity, which is so often neglected, is more important than the other four, so let's consider it in detail. The fifth *paccaya* is that which cajoles and entertains us, making us content, easing our anxiety and agitation, so that we are no longer hungry to the point of death. Amusing the heart, making it satisfied and pleased, is crucial. This is the mental *paccaya* or necessity. We might call it different names, such as entertainment or amusement. The important point is that whatever we call it, it must be right for the mind. It must be nourishment, food for the mind, just as the other four are food for the body.

Much of the time, worldly people think of the fifth necessity as a matter of sex. But we are interested in something different. Sex can entertain the mind, but now we are ready for Dhamma-Dhamma-Dhamma to be our amusement. This means we use appropriate means to amuse and satisfy us. When we are aware of correctness and are satisfied with it, when we feel proper and are content, the heart is entertained and the mind is amused. This sense of correctness and contentedness need not have anything to do with sex.

There is a building at Suan Mokkh called the "Theater of Spiritual Entertainments."[4] It was built to provide entertainment for the heart. It is full of pictures that not only teach Dhamma but also amuse and please. This is one form the fifth *paccaya* can take. We should get to know this type of fifth necessity whose nature is not sexual but Dhammic. Let's not follow the majority who ignore the fact that sex is caught up in endless complexities and difficulties and who still cling to sex as their fifth necessity.

In summary, it is important that we adjust our mode of living to fit the study and practice of *citta-bhāvanā*. Then it will be easy and convenient for us to study and practice successfully. We will discover the "new life" that is above and beyond the influence of positivism and negativism.[5] We will be discussing the details later, for this matter is very subtle. We can say that "new life" is above all problems and beyond all aspects of *dukkha*. It is free, liberated, and emancipated because we practice Dhamma with the support and aid of all five *paccayas*. Let's endeavor to gather all five correct and proper conditions for our Dhamma practice.

## PHYSICAL PREPARATIONS

Next, let's consider the immediate preparations for practicing *ānāpānasati*. First, we must choose a place that is suitable and appropriate for our practice. We select the best location available, knowing that we can never have a perfect situation. We try to find a place that is quiet and peaceful, where the conditions and weather are good and where there are no disturbances. But when good conditions are not available, we do the best we can with what we have. We must choose something, somewhere. We must be able to practice even while sitting on the train traveling from Bangkok. In this case, we can focus on the breath until we do not hear the noise of the wheels and do not feel the shaking as the train rattles over the rails. This shows that we can choose a location and use the conditions available to us in the best possible way.

We are not going to be defeated by circumstances, even on the train. Whether we have perfect conditions or not, we will make the best of them and do what we can. When we want to practice, we can use the sound of the train itself as a meditation object. Instead of the breath, the "clack-clack-clack" of the wheels on the rails can be our meditation object. In this way we cannot object to any location in the world, whether it is perfectly suitable or not. We will have no excuses regarding our choice of a proper location.

The next preliminary step is to prepare the body. Ideally, we need a body that is normal, free of disease, and without any respiratory or digestive abnormalities. More specifically, however, we can prepare the nose so that it functions smoothly and correctly. In ancient times, practitioners took clean lukewarm water in the palm of the hand, drew it up into the nose, and then blew the water out. If we do this two or three times, the nose will be clean and prepared, able to breathe well. The nose will then be much more sensitive to the breath. This is an example of getting our body ready.

### TIME AND TEACHER

The time of practice is also important. When we are determined to practice earnestly, we need to choose the most suitable and appropriate time possible. However, if we cannot find a good time, we accept whatever we can get. We do not have to be enslaved to a certain time of day. Whenever possible, we should choose a time when there are no distractions or disturbances. But when there is no time that is completely free of distractions, we use the best time available. Then the mind learns to be undistracted regardless of how many disturbances are occurring. Actually, we are training the mind to be undisturbed no matter what is happening around us. The mind will learn to be peaceful. We should not limit ourselves to any certain time when things must be just right, or we will never find it. Some people do this until they cannot find any time to meditate at all! That is not right. We must always be flexible and able to practice at any time.

The next consideration involves what is called an *ācāriya* (teacher, master). In truth, even in the old training systems, they did not talk much about an *ācāriya*. Such a person was called a "good friend" (*kalyāna-mitta*). It is correct to refer to this person as "friend." A friend is an advisor who can help us with certain matters. We should not forget, however, the basic principle that no one can directly help someone else. Nowadays everyone wants a teacher to supervise them! But here, a good friend is someone who has extensive personal experience and knowledge about the meditation practice, or whatever else it is we are striving to do. Although he or she is able to answer questions and explain some difficulties, it is not necessary for a friend to sit over us and supervise every breath. A good friend who will answer questions and help us work through certain obstacles is more than enough. To have such a *kalyāna-mitta* is one more thing to arrange.

## SITTING POSTURE

With regard to the actual activity of meditation itself, the first thing to discuss is the sitting posture. It is important to sit in a way that is both stable and secure, so that when the mind becomes semiconscious, we will not fall over. We should be able to sit just like a pyramid. A pyramid cannot fall over because it has a very solid base and sides that rise up into a central pinnacle. There is no way that it can fall down. Consider how long the pyramids in Egypt have been sitting! So we learn to sit like a pyramid. The best way is to sit cross-legged. Put your legs out in front of you, then pull the right foot up onto the left thigh and the left foot up onto the right thigh. If you have yet to try sitting this way, or are not even used to sitting on the floor, you may need some time to train the body to sit in such a posture. It is worth the effort. You can patiently, gradually train yourself to sit this way. Then you will never fall over, as it will be impossible to fall forwards, backwards, or sideways. From ancient times this way of sitting has been called "the lotus posture" (*padmāsana*).

It is also important to sit upright, with the vertebrae and spine in proper alignment, without any bends or curves. The vertebrae should sit snugly one on top of the other so that they fit together properly. This is what is normal for the body. The spine is a vital part of the nervous system, so we should sit erect in order to keep it straight and correct. This is good posture.

If you have never sat like this, it may be difficult at first. Nevertheless, it is important that you try to do it. The first time, you may be able only to fold your legs in front without crossing them. That is enough to begin. Later, put one leg on top of the other, crossing one leg. Eventually, you will be able to cross both legs in a "full lotus" position. This way of sitting is as compact as a pyramid and will not tip over when the mind is concentrated or half-concentrated. A straight spine is necessary because it stimulates the correct kind of breathing. If the spine is bent, there will be another kind of breathing. Therefore, we must try to straighten the spine, even if it is a little difficult at first.[6]

Next, consider the hands. The most comfortable and easiest placement is to let the hands fall onto the knees. Another way is to lay one hand on top of the other in the lap. This second position may be uncomfortable because the hands can become hot. If we rest them on the knees, they will not get hot. Some groups advise people to fold their hands in the lap with the thumbs touching in order to aid concentration. That is how they do it in China, and this position can also be good. You should choose whichever position seems most suitable for you. The hands will not heat up if you leave them on the knees. Or you can lay them in the lap if that is comfortable. Or you can press your thumbs together to increase concentration a bit. You can choose the placement that is best for you from among these different positions of the hands.

## COOL, CONCENTRATED EYES

Practitioners often ask, "Should we leave the eyes open or close them?" Many people believe that they must close their eyes, that they cannot meditate with open eyes. If you are serious about what you are doing and have a sufficiently strong mind, it is not difficult to practice with the eyes left open. Begin with the eyes open. Open them with the determination to gaze toward the tip of the nose. This is not impossible; it just takes a little effort. Gaze at the tip of the nose so that the eyes do not get involved with other things. When we close our eyes, we tend to grow sleepy, so be careful about closing the eyes. Also, when the eyes are closed, they tend to become warm and dry. Meditating with the eyes open will help us to stay awake and will keep the eyes cool and comfortable. Furthermore, this will help the mind to be concentrated; it will aid the development of *samādhi* (concentration or collectedness). As *samādhi* gradually develops, the eyes will naturally close by themselves. The eyelids will relax and drop shut on their own. This is nothing to worry about. The complete technique begins with the eyes open. Gaze at the tip of the nose until you develop *samādhi*, then the eyes will close on their own.

Practicing with the eyes open and gazing at the tip of the nose automatically produces a noticeable level of concentration. If we establish the entire mind in gazing at the tip of the nose, we will not see anything else. If we can do this, a certain level of *samādhi* is produced. We profit from having this much concentration right from the start. Merely look at the nose without seeing anything else. If all of the mind's attention is set on looking at the nose, then nothing else will be seen. This *samādhi* is not insignificant. Therefore, we should start with open eyes.

We are intent upon gazing at the nose, at feeling the nose, and at the same time we feel the body breathing. Both can be done concurrently. It may seem that both are being done at exactly the same moment, but they are not. There is nothing unnatural or supernatural about it. Because of the mind's great speed it is possible for the eyes to be gazing at the tip of the nose and to be aware of breathing in and breathing out at the same time. You can experience this for yourself.

## FOLLOWING THE BREATH WITH MINDFULNESS

Finally, we come to noting, contemplating, our breathing. In order to begin, we must develop *sati* (mindfulness or reflective awareness) by being mindful of each in-breath and out-breath. We train in *sati* by noting that we are about to breathe in or breathe out. Let the breathing continue comfortably and normally. Let it be natural. Do not interfere with it in any way. Then contemplate each breath with mindfulness. How are we breathing in? What is the out-breath like? Use *sati* to note the ordinary breath.

We first develop and train *sati* by using a technique called "following," or "chasing." We imagine the in-breath starting from the tip of the nose and ending at the navel. We imagine the out-breath starting at the navel and ending at the tip of the nose. In between these two points is the space through which the breath runs in and out. We contemplate with *sati* the properties of this movement in and out, from the tip of the nose to the navel and back again. Back and forth. Do not allow any gaps or lapses. This is the first lesson: contemplate the breath with *sati*.

Even though we are not medical students, we still know that the breath only goes into the lungs, that it does not go all the way down to the navel. Imagining that the breath ends at the navel is merely a useful convention; we do not hold it to be true. It is just an assumption based on our feeling and sensitivity of the movement of the breathing. When we breathe, we feel movement all the way down to the navel. We use that feeling as the basis of our practice and follow the breath between the tip of the nose and the navel.

The distinction as to whether it is *sati* that follows the breath in and out or whether *sati* forces the mind to follow the breath in and out is not important at this point. All that matters is to contemplate the breath as if chasing it, without ever losing it. The breath goes in and stops a moment. Then it comes out and pauses a moment. In and out, in and out, with short breaks in between. We must note everything and not let anything slip by. We do not allow empty spaces where the mind might wander but keep the mind constantly focused on the breathing in and out.

This is the first lesson to learn, the foundation for all the rest. It may not be so easy. Maybe it will take three days, three weeks, or three months until we are able to do it. This is the first step, the first task that we must accomplish. Here we are merely explaining the method of training; it is the practice that counts. You may not get very far in a ten-day course at Suan Mokkh or some other meditation center, but it is important to know what needs to be done and to get started doing it. Once you correctly understand the method, you can practice on your own until you are successful. So begin with this simple step: contemplate the breath as it moves between the nose and the navel without leaving any chances for the mind to wander elsewhere.

### MANY KINDS OF BREATH

As we practice "following," we have the opportunity to observe the various characteristics of the breath. For example, we can feel the long and the short duration of the breath. Thus, we learn naturally about the long breath and short breath. We can observe the coarse and fine nature of the breath. Further, we can observe its smoothness and bumpiness. Later, we will observe the reactions to these qualities. In this first step, however, we contemplate the different kinds of breath: long and short, coarse and fine, easy and uneasy. Begin to observe the various kinds by experiencing them with *sati*.

We must learn to observe in greater detail, that is, to observe the reaction or influence of each different kind of breathing. What reactions do they cause? How do they influence our awareness? For example, when each breath is long, how does this affect our awareness? What reactions do short breaths cause? What are the influences of coarse and fine breathing, of comfortable and uncomfortable breathing? We should observe the different types of breath and their various influences until we can distinguish clearly how the long and short breaths, coarse and fine breaths, and comfortable and uncomfortable breaths differ. We must learn to know the reactions to these various properties of the breath. Likewise, we must learn to know when these qualities influence our awareness, our sensitivity, our mind.

It is also important for us to note the effect or flavor of each kind of breath. The flavors that arise as different kinds of feeling are: happiness, unhappiness, *dukkha*, annoyance, and contentment. We observe and experience the flavors or effects caused by the long breath and the short breath, by the coarse breath and the fine breath, and by the easy breath and the uneasy breath. Find out why they have different flavors. For instance, we can see that the long breath gives a greater sense of peace and well-being; it has a happier taste than the short breath. Different kinds of breath bring different kinds of happiness. We learn to analyze and distinguish the various flavors that characterize the different kinds of breathing we have scrutinized.

Finally, we can discover the various causes that render our breathing either long or short. We gradually learn this by ourselves. What causes the breathing to be long? What kind of mood makes the breath long? What kind of mood makes it short? Thus, we also come to know the causes and conditions that make the breath long or short.

There is a method that we can use to regulate the breath in these beginning steps to make it longer or shorter. This technique is called "counting," and it trains us to change the length of our breathing. For example, as we inhale, we count from one to five. If during one breath we count at the same pace but from one to ten, that breath will lengthen accordingly. During an ordinary breath we only count to five. For a short breath we might count to three and that shortens the breath as we wish. We should always count at the same speed, for if we change the pace of counting, it will negate the effect of counting higher or lower. By counting, we can regulate the duration of each breath. By using this special training technique we can lengthen or shorten the breath. We do not have to use it all the time, but we can employ it occasionally to help us regulate the breath or to get to know it better. We can give it a try whenever we choose.

In this chapter, we have described various preparations for our practice and the actual establishment of mindfulness on breathing. This practice is the foundation for a more detailed examination of the four stages that were described in the first chapter. Some meditators may be satisfied with just this level of practice; it can be quite difficult in and of itself at the start. Nonetheless, let's continue our study of the first stage: contemplation of the body.

# 3

# Bodies of Breath

As we have mentioned before, altogether there are four groups that we must contemplate, each group corresponding to one of our four fundamental objects of study. Each group includes four steps, or *dhammas*; hence they may be called "tetrads." In all, therefore, there are four tetrads, or groups, each of which contains four steps. This makes a total of sixteen *dhammas*. Of these sixteen, the breath is directly contemplated in only two steps. The remaining fourteen steps focus on other objects.

The first of our four objects of study is *ānāpānasati* focused on the *kāya*. In this chapter we will examine the practice of the first two of the four steps of *ānāpānasati* focused on the *kāya*.

## *KĀYĀNUPASSANĀ*

In the *kāya* tetrad, or *kāyānupassanā* (contemplation of the body), we study and understand the breath. We learn to understand the different kinds of breath, their various qualities and characteristics, and the influences they produce. We get to know the breath in all aspects and from all angles in order for it to be correct.

To put it briefly, we must have correct *prāṇa*. *Prāṇa* is a Sanskrit word, the Pali equivalent is *pāṇa*. Ordinarily, this word means "life" or "life force" or "that which preserves and nurtures life." We must understand it correctly; our *prāṇa* should be healthy and correct. Then our lives will be correct. Thus, it is necessary to study the subject of the breath.

In India every style of yoga—and there are dozens of styles—has trainings involving the *prāṇa*. These trainings are called *prāṇāyāma*, which means "control of the *prāṇa*" or "breath control." To control the breath is to control life. When the *prāṇa* enters the body, it is called *āna* and when it leaves it is called *apāna*. The two words combined become *ānāpāna*, that is, the *prāṇa* enters and the *prāṇa* exits. To control the *prāṇa* is to control that which enters to preserve life.

Then we live a life that is fresh and cheerful, ready and fit for training and practice. Such *prāṇa* training can be found even in Buddhism.

*Prāṇāyāma* is the first subject of *ānāpānasati*. Although this may seem surprising, it does not contradict our principles at all. In fact, *ānāpānasati* is the equivalent of any system of yoga; indeed, it actually improves on all of them. This system of *kāyānupassanā* (contemplation on the body) takes up the *prāṇāyāma* of the Indian yogas and improves upon them in appropriateness and practicability.[7] Thus, our first item of study is this system of training known as *kāyānupassanā*.

If we adjust the *prāṇa*-body, so that it is good, healthy, and calm, it makes the flesh-body good, healthy, and calm as well. Calm and healthy *prāṇa* brings the greatest peace and well-being in this life. This is why we must understand both *kāya* (bodies): the flesh-body and the breath-body. Then we shall be able to cultivate the "good" until there is good peace and good calm. The word *good* here means "fit and proper to be used in performing duties and work."

The last item of this tetrad is calming the body-conditioner, that is, making the preservers of the body peaceful and calm. By calming the breath, which conditions the body, then the body too becomes tranquil. The *citta* will feel this tranquility and will also be calmed. When the *citta* is calm, it is ready to perform its further duties.

This is the subject matter of the *kāya*. It is important to note that the more you understand these facts, the more benefits this training will bring; you will become able to make this the best life possible. So we begin with learning about the *kāya* as the first tetrad.

## THE BUDDHA'S *PRĀṆĀYĀMA*

It is essential that we understand this profound truth: the *prāṇa*-body is the conditioner of the flesh-body. We ought to know that there are these two *kāya* or levels of *kāya*. We know about the first level, the flesh-body, but we hardly know the *prāṇa*-body at all. Therefore, it is very important to understand the *prāṇa*-body, as it can condition the flesh-body in beneficial ways. In India, the *prāṇāyāma* is considered to be the highest and most important subject for study. While different schools vary in their explanations and meanings for the *prāṇa*-body, all schools seek to regulate the *prāṇa*-body so that it conditions the flesh-body appropriately. We need to study and train the breath in order to use it to condition the flesh-body. Since we cannot regulate the flesh-body directly, we regulate it indirectly. We study the *prāṇa*-body and practice regulating it. By learning to regulate the *prāṇa*-body, we regulate the flesh-body, making it calm and peaceful.

We develop this knowledge through practice and training until we are able to regulate the *prāṇa*. In this way we gradually develop a good, healthy body that is ready for concentrating the *citta*. Both the body and mind are prepared to do their respective duties. The first tetrad, the *kāya*, has these characteristics, this objective and method of practice. We should examine this tetrad carefully. Is it necessary or not? Is it worth our time and effort to study and practice? If so, then we should wholeheartedly commit ourselves to this study and train in it until we are successful. This is the way to cultivate the best *prāṇāyāma*—Buddhist *prāṇāyāma*—through the practice of *vipassanā-bhāvanā* (the cultivation of insight or direct realization).

There are four steps in the practice of the *kāya* tetrad: knowing the long breath, knowing the short breath, knowing how the breath regulates the body, and contemplating the breath in order to calm the body. These four steps are not difficult if we sincerely observe and genuinely study in a scientific way.

Before the Buddha's time people practiced many types of *prāṇāyāma*. When Lord Buddha appeared, he too practiced *prāṇāyāma*; he then incorporated it into this system of contemplating the breath. And through this system of contemplating the breath, we regulate life and the body.

There are many advantages and benefits to *prāṇāyāma* that are not directly concerned with religion or Dhamma. These extra incentives may serve to interest you in *prāṇāyāma* or breath control and encourage you to manage it correctly. First, you can live longer through practicing *prāṇāyāma*. Or you can make yourself die immediately, even today, if you so wish. In fact, with the practice of *prāṇāyāma* you can die during any breath you choose. On the other hand, you can have a healthy breath and a good, healthy body with *prāṇāyāma*. You can play sports, drive a car, work in an office, or do whatever you choose if you regulate the breath or *prāṇa* in a way that is in accordance with your aims. You should know that these are some of the side-benefits of *ānāpānasati* outside the scope of religion or Dhamma proper.

## STEP ONE: THE LONG BREATH

Let's consider in more detail the first two steps of the first tetrad, the practice concerning the *kāya* (body). Having followed the instructions in the last chapter, we have developed a preliminary understanding of the breath. We know about the various properties of the breath: long duration, shortness, coarseness, fineness, easiness, and uneasiness. Our knowledge extends to the properties connected with the breath and how our mind reacts toward and is influenced by these properties. We even know how to control the length of each breath. The next step is to enter a course of training with the breathing. We begin with the long breath.

The first lesson is the contemplation of the long breath. Having learned how to make the breath long and to keep it long, we are able to breathe long whenever we need to. In this first lesson, we will study exclusively the nature of the long breath. When a breath is long, how pleasant is it? Is it natural and ordinary? What kinds of calmness and happiness arise? In what ways is it different from a short breath? We begin by studying just the long breath to find out its properties, qualities, influence, and flavor. We should sit and investigate only the long breath. This is lesson one: understanding all matters connected to long breathing.

Finally, we observe how the body works in relation to the long breath. How does the body move when there is a long inhalation? In what places does the body expand? Where does it contract? When there is the deepest possible long breath, does the chest expand or contract? Does the abdomen expand or contract? These are things to examine. As you observe, you may learn that the process happens differently than you might have thought. Most people have the simple idea that when we breathe in, the chest expands, and when we breathe out, the chest contracts. In studying the breath carefully, however, we find that in taking a very long inhalation, the abdomen will contract and the chest will expand. We find the reverse of what common sense teaches. Thus, we investigate the very long breath, the longest possible breath, to see what changes occur. We do not take anything for granted but instead learn these basic facts for ourselves.

In order to know the nature of the long breath, we study all the secrets and attributes of the long breath. We are able to contemplate its long duration, learning to protect and maintain it. In fact, we become expert in all matters concerned with the long breath. Practicing with the long breath is lesson one.

It is extremely important that we learn the interrelationship between each type of breath and the body. We shall find there is a very close interconnection between them. As we learn the effects that the long breath has on the body, we discover the happiness and comfort the long breath brings. Further, we come to understand more deeply the secret of the two *kāya*: the breath-body and the flesh-body. We can observe this even at this early stage, although we will not discuss it specifically until step three. Still, in this lesson, we should begin to realize how the breath and the body are interconnected. Therefore, when breathing long, or in any way, we observe how the rest of the body is affected. We learn in a deeper way, through personal experience rather than through thinking, that the breath is intimately associated with the body.

### STEP TWO: THE SHORT BREATH

Our second lesson concerns the short breath. We practice this step in exactly the same way as we practiced the long breath, only now we focus on the short breath. Whatever we learned about the long breath, we shall learn the equivalent facts about the short breath.

For instance, we observe and feel immediately that the long breath brings ease and comfort while the short breath leads to abnormality, that is, uneasiness, agitation, and discomfort. Thus, through our ability to regulate the breath, we know how to make the body either comfortable or uncomfortable. We need to know the complementary differences between the two kinds of breath as clearly as possible. So here we are particularly interested in the short breath. We study everything, every aspect, every property of the short breath until we know it as extensively as we know the long breath. Although the two kinds of breath have opposite natures, our way of studying them is identical.

Of special interest is the observation that when we breathe long, the breath is fine, and when we breathe short, the breath is rough. Once we learn to make the breath fine or coarse as we wish, we can use this ability to our advantage. The benefit is that the fine breath will calm our body. It becomes cool. When we wish to cool down our body, we bring out the fine breath. When we require the fine breath, we simply make the breath longer. This is one of the fine points we need to study.

Another example is that when we are angry, the breath becomes short. When the breath is short, the body is disturbed. If we make the breath long, our anger will not continue. When we are angry, the breath is short and rough, and the body is rough. We can drive away such anger by breathing long. The body will be relaxed, and the anger will disappear. This is an example of the many different interactions and relationships between the breath, the body, and the mind. It is important that we understand the relationship and differences between long and short breathing. We must experience this relationship and feel it for ourselves so that we become experts.

### BREATHING AWAY EMOTIONS

Let's summarize these first steps: it is possible to regulate, control, limit, and manage the emotions by using the breath. We can make the emotions correct, useful, and beneficial through the breath. We develop the ability to control the breath itself through knowledge we have gained about the breath. If we train our breathing, we can control our emotions, that is, we can cope with the happiness and pain in our lives. We should practice until we feel this; our practice is not complete until we can see this clearly.

When you are sitting in meditation and a mosquito bites you, you may develop an evil emotion. How can you get rid of it? To drive it away, improve the breath. Make the breath long, make it fine, make it chase away that wicked emotion. This is the best method to solve such problems and is another example of the beneficial knowledge and useful abilities that we are learning.

The topics and facts to be studied in the first lesson about the long breath and in the second lesson about the short breath are the same. The only difference is that everything is complementary. The number and type of things to study are equal, but the differences between long and short breathing lead to complementary sets of facts.

This completes our discussion of the first two lessons of the first tetrad. Two more lessons of this tetrad remain to be considered. Please practice what you have read as you prepare for what comes next.

# 4

# Calming the *Kāya*

NEXT, WE WILL CONSIDER steps three and four of the first tetrad, that is, the remaining steps concerned with the *kāya* (body).

### STEP THREE: EXPERIENCING ALL BODIES

In step three, the aim is to experience all *kāya*, all bodies. The essence of this step is to feel all bodies while breathing in and breathing out. While practicing the earlier steps of *ānāpānasati*, we began to observe that the breath conditions our flesh-and-blood body. This next step, therefore, does not involve anything new; we merely investigate this fact more profoundly, clearly, and carefully than before. We contemplate in a deeper way that there are two *kāya* (bodies). We should continuously observe this while breathing in and breathing out.

The practitioner will recall that the breath is the conditioner of the flesh-body. Here, we are distinguishing between two entities, both of which are called *kāya* (body). The breath is a body in that it is a group, a collection. The flesh-body is also a *kāya* because it too is a group or collection. Thus, there are two groups, two bodies. One group is the breath that conditions the flesh-body group. We should analyze this experience to see clearly that there are two groups and that they condition each other. Contemplate this thoroughly until it becomes obvious.

The meaning of the word *body* includes the idea of a *group*. In the original Pali language, Lord Buddha used this word *kāya* in expressing, for example, "*sabbakāyaṃpaṭisaṃveti*" (experiencing all bodies). In Thai, *kāya* comes from the Pali *kāya* and can also mean "group, pile, heap, division." This term can be applied not only to our human forms; it can refer to other things as well. For instance, in Pali a squad of soldiers is a *kāya* of soldiers. *Kāya* means "group, heap, collection"; we should not understand it only in terms of flesh-bodies. The breath is also called *kāya* or group. We must correctly understand the meaning of *kāya* in order to know what is meant by "experiencing all bodies." Then we can understand both the breath-body group and the flesh-body group.

The specific aim of this third step is to come to understand (1) that there are two groups and (2) that one group conditions, nourishes, and supports the other group. The breath-body group nourishes the flesh-body group. Actually, we have experienced this since the beginning of our *ānāpānasati* practice. Earlier, we learned that when the breath is coarse, the flesh-body becomes aggravated, and when the breath is fine, the body calms down. We have observed these facts while practicing steps one and two. In this step, we scrutinize this fact until these two groups become utterly clear. One group conditions and nourishes the other. We should know clearly the difference between them.

### THE THREE MEANINGS OF *SANKHĀRA*

We are gradually acquiring the inner, mental experience that these two bodies condition each other. The body that is the causal conditioner is given the name *kāya-sankhāra* (body-conditioner) to distinguish it from the one affected by the conditioning, the "conditioned body." We should work on this fact in the mind to see if it is physically tangible. Observe the one group as it conditions and nurtures the other. See them arise together, fall together, coarsen together, become fine together, grow comfortable together, and become uncomfortable together. Realize how intimately they are connected. This is what is meant by "seeing all bodies." Watch both bodies together and see them condition each other. This is valuable for seeing truth more extensively, even for realizing *anattā*. In observing this interrelationship, we learn that what is occurring is merely a natural process of conditioning. There is no *attā*, no self, no soul involved. Although it is beyond the specific objective of this step, such an understanding can have the highest benefit. For now, however, our purpose in understanding this conditioning is to be able to calm the flesh-body by regulating the breath-body.

Let us discuss all the meanings of the term *sankhāra*, a very common and important word in the Pali scriptures. We may encounter problems because of the different uses and meanings of the word *sankhāra*. Language, at times, can be uncertain and unreliable. The single word *sankhāra* can mean "conditioner," the cause that conditions; it can mean "condition," the result of the action of conditioning; and it can mean "conditioning," the activity or process of conditioning. We use the same word for the subject of the conditioning, "the concocter," as well as the object, "the concoction." We even use it for the activity, "the concocting," itself. This may be a bit confusing, so we should remember that *sankhāra* has three meanings. The correct meaning depends on the context. This knowledge will be valuable in our further studies.

You should study the three meanings of *sankhāra* in your body. There is no need to study it in books or in a theoretical way. The body itself is a *sankhāra*. It has been conditioned by a variety of causes and by the many elements of which it is formed. Thus, it is a *sankhāra* in the meaning of "condition." Once this body exists, it causes the arising of other things, such as thoughts, feelings, and actions. These thoughts and actions could never happen without the body. Thus, it is a "conditioner" because it causes other actions. Lastly, in this flesh-body *sankhāra* of ours, the process of conditioning goes on constantly. We can discover all three aspects of the word *sankhāra* within this very body. If you study the meaning of *sankhāra* in this comprehensive way, you will find it possible to realize more and more profound Dhamma.

### EXPERIENCING *SANKHĀRA*

In step three, "experiencing all bodies"—experiencing both the breath and this flesh-body—each of these three meanings is practiced. First, we contemplate the flesh-body as that which is conditioned by the breath. Then we observe the breath as the conditioner of the flesh-body. Lastly, we observe the activity of conditioning that always exists simultaneously between the breath and the flesh-body. Thus, in the practice of step three we see the conditioner, the condition, and the process of conditioning. This conditioning of the body is the physical level of *sankhāra*; we have yet to see the process at work on the mental level. Step three is the work of seeing these three elements together, simultaneously and continuously, within the mind. In this way we see everything concerning the term, especially as it relates to the *kāya* and its activity.

When we have plainly and clearly understood *sankhāra* as explained above, we will be able to experience all three of these meanings of *sankhāra* together in one moment. Even during the span of only one inhalation or one exhalation, in just a single stroke of the breath, we can experience all three elements. If we are successful, then we will have "fully experienced the *kāya-sankhāra*" (body-conditioner) and will have completed step three.

The essence of practicing step three is to know that there are two *kāya* and to regulate one *kāya* through the other. That is, we regulate the flesh-body through the breath-body. Once we have understood this clearly and are convinced by our experience of this process with each in-breath and out-breath, then we have realized success in our practice of step three.

### STEP FOUR: CALMING THE BREATH

Once we know that we can regulate the flesh-body with the breath-body, we begin to practice step four. Lord Buddha described step four as "calming the body-conditioner" (*passambhayaṁ kāya-sankhāraṁ*). Step four is calming the body-conditioner (*kāya-sankhāra*) while breathing in and calming the body-conditioner while breathing out. This means that as we inhale and exhale we make the body-conditioner (breath) calmer and calmer. Let's explore this in more detail.

"Calming the body-conditioner" refers to calming the breath-body. In step four, the aim of our practice is to calm the breath; using various techniques which are available to us, we make it fine and peaceful. If we can calm the breath, the results will be very interesting and powerful. First of all, the flesh-body will simultaneously become very gentle, relaxed, and tranquil. Then there will also arise a calming of the mind. There will be other results as well, which we will discuss at a later point. The immediate lesson is to calm the breath; managing the breath is the first point to be considered in the practice of step four.

### FIVE SKILLFUL TRICKS

In practicing step four, there are various methods, or techniques—we could even call them tricks—to use in calming the breath. It is important to note that these are a higher order of methods that we use over more crude and foolish techniques. Thus, we call them "skillful means." The tricks, or skillful means, to use on the breath come in five stages:

1. following the breath;
2. guarding the breath at a certain point;
3. giving rise to an imaginary image at that guarding point;
4. manipulating these images in such a way as to gain power over them; and
5. selecting one image and contemplating it in a most concentrated way until the breath becomes truly calm and peaceful.

These are our five techniques, or skillful means: following, guarding, raising a mental image, playing with the different mental images, and choosing one image to be the specific object of *samādhi* (concentration, collectedness) until there is complete calmness.

The first stage—following or chasing—we have actually been doing from the beginning. We use hunting or following with the long and short breaths. Now, we merely repeat or review it until we become skilled at following the breath. This does not require further explanation since we have already done it many times in steps one, two, and three.

The second technique is guarding: choosing one point along the breath's path and watching or guarding the breath there. We no longer follow the breath, but the results are the same as if we continued to do so. This *citta*, this *sati*, is not allowed to go anywhere; it must stay at the chosen point. It guards the breath passing in and passing out; hence, the results are equivalent to following, except that guarding is more subtle.

Generally, we use the furthest point on the nose where the breath makes contact, usually at the tip. This point is the easiest and simplest to guard, unless you have a hooked nose that comes down low and a high upper lip. Then you might feel the breath's touch just above the upper lip. For each of us the point will be in a different place, depending on the shape and structure of our nose and lip.

Find the place where you can observe the breath most easily. If you have difficulty finding it while breathing normally, take a few deep, strong breaths, and the spot will become obvious. The exact location is not important; just find that point on your nose, or even on the upper lip, where you feel the breath most clearly. Once you find it, guard that point as the breath passes in and out. The mind, the *sati*, stays right at that point and contemplates the breath as it goes in and out. Just breathe in and breathe out with the mind guarding that point; this is stage two in our series of skillful means.

We can observe that when we do not note the breath and just let it go as it pleases, it has a certain feel. The breath becomes finer and gentler as soon as we begin to note it, even when merely following it. It adjusts itself and becomes subtler in order to deceive us. It plays tricks like this. Then, when we stop chasing and start to guard the breath at a specific point on the nose, the breath calms down even more. You can verify this through your own experience.

## A MENTAL IMAGE APPEARS

If we create a mental image (*nimitta*) at the guarding point, the breath will be further refined and calmed. This mental image is not real, but imaginary. It is created by the *citta*, it is mind-made. You can close your eyes and "see" it, you can open your eyes and still "see" it. The image is like a hallucination the mind creates by itself to calm the breath. To do this the mind must be subtle. The breath, indeed all the faculties, must be refined in order for a mental image to arise. The breath must become finer and calmer until the image is created.

The mental image can be any shape or form, depending on what is appropriate for the body of each person. Some people might create a sphere—red, white, green, or any color. The mental image can be a candle flame, or a puff of cotton, or a wisp of smoke. It can look like the sun, or the moon, or a star. Even the image of a spider's web glimmering in the sunlight is within the abilities of the mind's creative powers. The kind of image depends on the one who creates it. The mind merely inclines in a certain way and the image arises by itself. It is a purely mental phenomenon that has no physical reality. The third technique is complete when we are able to create a mental image at the guarding point.

Skillful means number four is to change the image or alternate between images according to our requirements. We can change from one image to another, changing them in all the ways that we wish. How is this possible? Because the mind creates the images in the first place, it has the ability to change them, to manipulate them, to play with them. This can all be done easily; it is well within the mind's capabilities. At the same time, as we do this, we are developing our ability to master the mind in increasingly subtle and powerful ways.

Because we can now control the mind more than before, the *citta* automatically grows more subtle and refined by itself. The *citta* becomes more and more calm until eventually we are able to calm the mind completely. We merely control the images, changing them according to the mind's tendencies. Depending on the mind's inclination, we can experiment with changing the images in ways that calm the breath more and more. Although this is nothing more than a trick, it is a more advanced trick that enables us to have greater influence over the mind. Then the breath calms down automatically. The breath must become calmer for us to manipulate the images. Although the mind also calms down, the emphasis at the present is on calming the breath. The fourth technique is controlling the mental images as we wish.

## THE FINAL IMAGE

If we observe the process of calming, we watch and see that when we train in the prescribed way, the breath automatically becomes more refined and calms down by itself. When the breath is calmed, the flesh-body automatically calms down accordingly. Now when the body calms down, this has an effect on the mind. The *citta* becomes calm in proportion to the calming of the body, but this calming of the mind is the aim of a later step. Here, by calming the breath in this most refined way, the body will calm down accordingly. So we observe the calming process while practicing this step.

The fifth skillful means is choosing the single most appropriate *nimitta* (image) and not changing it again. We choose the one image that is most fitting and proper, and then contemplate it with our full attention in order to develop a complete measure of *samādhi* (mental stability and integration). We should choose an image that is soothing, relaxing, and easy to focus on. The image should not stir up thoughts and emotions or contain any special significance or meaning. A mere white point or dot will suffice.

Indeed, the best kind of image is neutral. A colored image will brew thoughts and feelings, as will attractive, interesting, fancy, or complicated images. Some people like to use a picture of the Buddha as their *nimitta*, but this can cause thinking and distraction; the thoughts will merely follow the image that is seen, rather than easing into stillness. Therefore, we should take an image that has no meaning or mental associations and is natural. A white spot is perfectly suitable; so is a tiny spot of light. Some people prefer a Buddha image or whatever suits their fancy, but we do not. We take a spot that is easy to contemplate and does not stir up any thoughts. We choose such an image and focus all of the mind on it, for the purpose of developing concentration. We focus on just this simple point so that the *citta* does not wander anywhere else. The *citta* gathers together on this single spot. Concentrating everything on this one point is the fifth of our skillful means.

## PERFECT CONCENTRATION

We should select an object (*nimitta*) to contemplate that is the most appropriate for the mind. Ordinarily, the mind is scattered, spreading and radiating outward in all directions. Now, we must turn inward onto one focal point to end that outward flowing. In Pali this state is called *ekaggatā*, which means "to have a single peak, focus, or apex." Everything gathers at this single focus. We have found an image that is the most appropriate—a tiny central point— and now the mind focuses in on it. The mental flow is collected at this point in the same way that a magnifying glass collects the sun's rays and focuses them into a single point powerful enough to ignite a flame. This example illustrates the power that is harnessed when all of the mind's energy is gathered into one point. Once the mind focuses on the object we have chosen, its radiance gathers there and becomes *ekaggatā*: one-pointed, one-peaked, one-pinnacled.

When the mind is one-pointed, there are no other feelings, thoughts, or objects of that mind. There remain only the *jhānaṅga* (factors of *jhāna*). At the first level of one-pointedness there are five factors. At this first level the mind is still coarse enough to perform the function of contemplating the object. The mind noting its object is called *vitakka*. The mind experiencing that object is called *vicāra*. The mind is satisfied or contented (*pīti*) because of the *vitakka* and *vicāra*. And once there is *pīti*, the feeling of joy (*sukha*) arises at the same instant. Lastly, one-pointedness of mind (*ekaggatā*) continues as before. Thus, the mind on this level of *samādhi* (concentration) has five factors: noting (*vitakka*), experiencing (*vicāra*), contentment (*pīti*), joy (*sukha*), and one-pointedness (*ekaggatā*). These five factors indicate that the mind has entered the first level of perfect *samādhi*. This kind of concentrated awareness does not include any thinking, yet these five activities of the mind occur. We call them factors of *jhāna*. If all five are present, then we are successful in having perfect *samādhi*, although only the first stage. That sounds strange—perfect, but only the first stage of perfection.

## AT THE PEAK

Let's take a closer look at *ekaggatā*. This Pali word is commonly translated as "one-pointedness," although literally, the Pali term means "to have one single (*eka*) peak (*agga*; Thai, *yod*)." The Thai word *yod* (rhymes with *laud*) can mean either the very top, peak, apex, or pinnacle of something, such as a mountain or a pyramid, or the new tip or growing point of a plant. The word *point* in English does not have quite the same meaning, as a point can be anywhere, off to the side or even down very low. This is why Pali uses the word *agga* (peak, summit, or zenith). *Ekaggatā* is like being the peak of a pyramid. It would not be proper for such a mind to be at some low point; it must be on a high level. The one-pointed mind is gathered together from low levels up to one high point or peak. This is the proper meaning of *ekaggatā*.

We should not worry, however, if at first the mind collects itself at a focal point that may not be the highest. It is a start. Whenever there is *ekaggatā*, it is the beginning of something most useful; whenever there is some *ekaggatā*, there is *samādhi*. In our practice of step four of *ānāpānasati*, it is not necessary to enter *jhāna* completely. In the practice of *ānāpānasati* these very refined levels of concentration are not necessary. We need only to have a sufficient and appropriate level of concentration to continue with our practice: that is, enough *samādhi* that feelings of *pīti* and *sukha* (contentment and happiness) are also present. We shall need the feelings of *pīti* and *sukha* in the next steps of our study. If we can progress further into *jhāna*, into the material absorptions (*rupa-jhāna*), that will be useful; it will make the next steps easier. But even if we do not reach *jhāna*, as long as some feelings of *pīti* and *sukha* are present, we are doing fine. With any luck, that will not prove to be too difficult.

When the feelings *pīti* and *sukha* are strong enough for the mind to feel them clearly, there is sufficient concentration to go on to step five. If you enter the first, second, third, or fourth *rupa-jhāna*, it is better still. But sufficient *samādhi* to experience *pīti* and *sukha* distinctly is enough for step four.

### IT'S EASY WHEN…

If you apply the method correctly, this practice is not difficult. If you have been reading carefully, then you understand the proper way to do this practice. If you follow the technique correctly, it will not be too difficult. You might even finish in a short time. If you do not practice according to the method, then it may be very difficult. You may never finish. It could take three days or three weeks for some, three months or even three years for others. Who can say?

If you are still at the beginning, working on step one, this does not mean you should not pay attention to the instructions about step four. If you do not know what to do, then it will be very difficult to practice when the time comes. Instructions are given as clearly as possible, so that you will understand the proper way to do this practice. Many people, however, do not like to follow instructions. They prefer to mix everything up with their own ideas and opinions. They like to make a hodgepodge out of things they read and hear from different places. If you want to make this practice successful and easy for yourself, you should follow these instructions, which explain the most proper and efficient way of using this technique.

Practicing according to the method is not difficult; not following the technique brings many difficulties. Therefore, if you learn the correct method and apply it, you will achieve the expected results. Beyond that, there is nothing else to do except repeat these steps many times until you can very quickly calm the breath and the body. You should practice until these steps require no effort and you have become well-versed in these activities.

We should not forget: in every step, in every stage and interval of the practice, we must note the breathing in and breathing out. This is the background and foundation of our *sati*. This is how to be supremely mindful. If we note the inhalations and exhalations at each stage of practice, we will meet with success in the first tetrad of *ānāpānasati*. This is the theoretical background of *ānāpānasati* and the principles on which we practice it.

This completes our discussion of the first tetrad of *ānāpānasati*, that is, the four steps concerning the *kāya* (body). The next chapter deals with the *vedanā* (feelings) and the tetrad, or four steps, concerning them.

# 5

# Mastering the *Vedanā*

IN THIS CHAPTER, we will discuss the second tetrad of *ānāpānasati*, which deals with the feelings. It is called *"vedanānupassanā"* (contemplation of feeling). The first two steps of this tetrad take *pīti* (contentment) and *sukha* (joy) as the subjects of our detailed examination and study. This practice develops out of the practice of the previous step. Once the body-conditioner, the breath, is calmed, feelings of *pīti* and *sukha* appear. We then take *pīti* and *sukha* as the next objects of our practice.

If we calm the *kāya-sankhāra* (body-conditioner) to the extent of entering *jhāna* (the first *jhāna* and so forth), then *pīti* and *sukha* will be full and complete as factors of *jhāna*. However, if we are unable to reach *jhāna* and are only able to calm the body-conditioner partially, there will likely be a degree of *pīti* and *sukha* present proportionate to the extent of that calming. Thus, even those practitioners who are unable to bring about *jhāna* can still manage enough *pīti* and *sukha* to practice these steps.

*Pīti* (contentment) arises from our successfully inducing *samādhi* in the previous steps, when we calmed the body-conditioner, or breath. Contentment or satisfaction arises with this success. Once there is contentment, happiness (*sukha*) will surely follow. Joy arises out of satisfaction. Thus, it is possible for us to experience sufficient *pīti* and *sukha* to be able to practice steps five and six.

## PĪTI IS NOT PEACEFUL

Next, we observe that there are different levels to *pīti*, such as contentment, satisfaction, and rapture. We must know these energetic gradations of *pīti*. Most importantly, we should be aware that *pīti* is not peaceful. There is a kind of excitement or disturbance in *pīti*; only when it becomes *sukha* is it tranquil. *Pīti* has varying levels, but all are characterized as stimulating, as causing the *citta* to tremble and shake. *Sukha* is the opposite; it calms and soothes the mind. This is how *pīti* and *sukha* differ.

Step one of the second tetrad, "experiencing *pīti*" (*pīti-paṭsaāvedi*), consists of contemplating *pīti* every time we breathe in and breathe out. We must keep watching until we find the *pīti* that has arisen from calming the body-conditioner. Find out what this feeling is like. Fully experience it. Take it as the new object for the mind to contemplate. The *citta* is absorbed in contemplating it the same as if there was *ekaggatā*. The mind is absorbed with the single object, *pīti*.

Throughout our practice we have contemplated a number of objects: the long breath, the short breath, all bodies, and calming the bodies. Now we switch to *pīti*. This *pīti* has stimulating power. It makes the mind quiver, shake, and tremble. It should be easy to understand the various degrees of *pīti* through the different English words we can use. How stimulating is contentment? To what degree is satisfaction stimulating? And how stimulating is rapture? We must observe and find out for ourselves. The mind focuses upon *pīti* and fully experiences it with every inhalation and exhalation. This is the essence of the practice of step five.

Briefly, we breathe, and we experience *pīti* with every breath. Breathing in and out, we fully experience this feeling of contentment and, simultaneously, are aware of each in-breath and each out-breath. There is a very pleasant feeling of well-being when this step is being practiced. This work is fun to do; it is a most enjoyable lesson.

## STUDY THE FLAVOR OF *PĪTI*

In each moment that we breathe with the experience of *pīti*, we are simultaneously studying and training. Earlier, we trained and studied while breathing long, breathing short, and so forth. Now, we study and train as we experience *pīti* in the mind. What is *pīti* like? Is it heavy? Is it light? How coarse is it? How subtle? This can be called "knowing its flavor." In particular, investigate the influence its flavor has on the mind and on the thoughts. Study in order to understand the nature of *pīti*, just as we studied to understand the nature of the breath during the practice of the previous tetrad. This is how to practice this step.

Most important, study and observe the power *pīti* has over the mind. What influence does *pīti* have on the mind and thoughts? Carefully observe the mind when *pīti* is not present. Once *pīti* arises, what is the *citta* like? What is the effect of an abundance of *pīti*? How is the mind when there is only minimal *pīti*? When *pīti* is intense, as in rapture, how much greater is the stimulation to the mind? See how the coarsest kinds of *pīti* differ from the medium levels and the finest types. Then, see how their influence upon the mind differs. This is the crucial point of this step of practice.

Finally, we realize that *pīti* stimulates the mind in a coarse way; it lacks a refined and subtle effect like *sukha*. In this step, understand the nature, facts, and secrets of this phenomenon known as *pīti*. Observe its relationship to the mind until the entire experience is completely familiar.

### *SUKHA* SOOTHES THE MIND

In the second step of this second tetrad—or step six overall—"experiencing *sukha*" (*sukha-paṭisaāvedi*), we contemplate *sukha* (happiness) with every inhalation and exhalation. We focus on *sukha* as arising out of *pīti*. When *pīti* has finished stimulating the *citta* in its coarse way, *pīti* loses energy. That is, it calms down and transforms into *sukha*. These two feelings are very different; *sukha* does not stimulate or excite; it calms down and soothes. Here we contemplate *sukha* as the agent that makes the *citta* tranquil. Usually *pīti* obscures *sukha*, but when *pīti* fades away, *sukha* remains. The coarse feeling gives way to calm. Taste the tranquil flavor of *sukha* with every inhalation and exhalation. This is the gist of step six.

As we contemplate *sukha* within the mind, our method of studying and training is identical to our practice with the breath and *pīti*. How light is *sukha*? How heavy? How coarse is it? How subtle? How does *sukha* flavor awareness and experience? In Thai and Pali we use the word *drink* to describe this experiencing. We drink the flavor of *sukha* while breathing in and breathing out, at the same time studying its nature and truth.

When the power of *pīti* is present, the breath is rough. When the influence of *sukha* is present, the breath is fine. Moreover, when *pīti* manifests its power, the flesh-body is coarse. When *sukha* manifests its influence, the body calms down and becomes subtle. There are similar effects on the *citta* as well. When *pīti* shows its power, it disturbs the mind proportionately, whereas the influence of *sukha* calms and relaxes the mind. That the two feelings are opposites is what we must observe with every in-breath and out-breath.

To summarize, once *pīti* and *sukha* arise, they have different effects upon the breath. *Pīti* will make the breath coarse, while *sukha* will make it calm. They also have different effects upon the body: *pīti* makes it coarse or agitated, while *sukha* soothes it. Finally, they have different effects upon the mind. The presence of *pīti* excites the mind, while the presence of *sukha* calms it. When you can experience this distinction directly, rather than through thought, you will have met with success in the practice of this step.

It is possible to experience some difficulties on this step. While we are contemplating *sukha*, *pīti* might interfere. It may predominate such that the feeling of *sukha* disappears. Therefore, we maintain that feeling of *sukha* for as long as needed to prevent *pīti* from arising. *Pīti* is much stronger and coarser than *sukha*. If *pīti* interferes, the contemplation of *sukha* is ruined and real tranquility will not arise. Superb effort in our contemplation of *sukha* is needed to ensure that it does not fade away. We should not let any other feelings interfere. In this step we should feel saturated with happiness, certainly a wonderful way to meet with success in the practice of step six.

### EXPERIENCING THE MIND-CONDITIONER

Now we come to step seven: "experiencing the mind-conditioner" (*citta-sankhāra-paṭsaāvedi*). If we have successfully completed step six, then we are familiar with the feelings of *pīti* and *sukha*. What does the arising of *pīti* do to the *citta*? How does the arising of *sukha* influence the *citta*? What kind of thoughts does *pīti* condition? And what thoughts does *sukha* condition? We have noted and scrutinized these effects since steps five and six. Once we come to step seven, it is easy to realize, "Oh, *pīti* and *sukha* are mind-conditioners." These *vedanā* are mind-conditioners in the same way that the breath is the body-conditioner. The method of study and observation is the same in this step as in step three.

We have observed that *pīti* is coarse and excited, whereas *sukha* is fine and peaceful. Thus, when *pīti* conditions a thought, that thought is coarse. On the other hand, when a thought arises through *sukha*, that thought is calm and tranquil. Thus, we realize the way that the *vedanā* condition thoughts. We learn that feelings condition both coarse thoughts and subtle thoughts. This activity is called "conditioning the mind."

When *pīti* is strong, it causes trembling in the body. If it is very strong, the body might even dance or bounce with joy. This feeling is coarse and powerful. On the other hand, *sukha* is calming, soothing, and relaxing. We learn that the characteristics of *pīti* and *sukha* are very different. When *pīti* dominates the mind, it is impossible to think subtle thoughts. We feel a tingling all over; it makes the hair stand up all over the body. So we need to be able to control *pīti*. However, *sukha* has advantages in that it leads to tranquil, refined states; it can cause subtle and profound thoughts. These two feelings might be called opponents or foes, but this does not really matter, for we have learned how to regulate them. We can control them by training according to the method of step seven. This is called "understanding the *citta-sankhāra* sufficiently."

## FRIENDS AND FOES

It is important that we now observe and understand a different secret: these two feelings must arise together. That is, if we are not contented or satisfied, happiness cannot occur. Contentment gives rise to happiness; joy arises from satisfaction. Contentment and satisfaction are the group of stimulating, pleasant feelings called *pīti*. Although happiness and joy belong in the group of soothing feelings, they cannot exist without satisfaction. We observe that where there is happiness, satisfaction must always arise first. *Pīti* leads the way. We are satisfied when we experience success; we get excited and disturbed by that success. Once *pīti* loses strength, when the mind gets tired of agitation and excitement, then *sukha* remains. The feeling calms down. So the two are comrades while at the same time opposing each other; they are comrades in that they must arise together. There must first be contentment for there to be joy. We need to be careful about this, acting toward these two in an extremely subtle and refined way. It is an art, a spiritual art of controlling *pīti* and *sukha* so that they benefit our lives. This is the secret that we ought to know concerning *pīti* and *sukha*.

We have discovered that *pīti* is a foe of *vipassanā*, whereas *sukha*, happiness-joy, is a friend, a supporter. *Vipassanā* means "seeing clearly," having direct insight into the truth of *aniccaā* (impermanence), *dukkhaā* (unsatisfactoriness), and *anattā* (not-self). We require a very refined mind to realize *aniccaā*, *dukkhaā*, and *anattā* through *vipassanā*. Should *pīti* arise, *vipassanā* is impossible. The mind becomes clouded and restless. *Pīti* must be driven away, for it is the enemy of *vipassanā*, that is, of clear, subtle mental vision. However, *sukha* is quite the opposite. *Sukha* soothes and calms, making the mind active and ready for *vipassanā*. For this reason, we must acquire the ability to regulate *pīti* and *sukha*.

We have realized that feelings (*pīti* and *sukha*) are mind-conditioners. When *pīti* conditions the *citta*, it is coarse and its thoughts are coarse; both the mind and thoughts are coarse. When *sukha* conditions or supports the *citta*, it is subtle and tranquil, and its thoughts are subtle and tranquil. Both feelings condition the mind, but from different angles. The *vedanā* are conditioners of the *citta*; thus they get the name "mind-conditioner" (*citta-sankhāra*).

We contemplate this fact in the mind every time we breathe in and breathe out. This is the practice of step seven.

## Calming the Feelings

Step eight is "calming the mind-conditioner" (*passambhayaā citta-sankhārā*) while breathing in and breathing out. We make the *citta-sankhāra*, the *vedanā*, calm and peaceful by lessening their energy while breathing in and breathing out. There are two approaches for us to use: the *samādhi* (concentration) method and the *paññā* (wisdom) method.

## The Concentration Method

We can calm *pīti's* impulse with the *samādhi* method, in which we develop a higher level of concentration that removes *pīti* and *sukha* from what is felt. As we have only just begun our training, we are probably not yet able to do this. Still, we should know that these feelings can be driven away by developing a higher level of *samādhi*, such as the third or fourth *jhāna*. Or alternatively, we can lessen the energy of *pīti* by bringing another kind of thought into the mind to intervene and suppress that satisfied feeling. Either technique uses the power of *samādhi*. Generally, it is not necessary to drive away *sukha*. In fact, we ought to preserve it as a support for further practice. Here, our objective is to control *pīti* with *samādhi* techniques, either by changing the mind's object or by having a higher degree of concentration or *jhāna*. Either method will calm down *pīti*.

Another possibility is to bring in the true meaning of the word *samādhi* to drive away *pīti*. The real meaning of *samādhi* is "having *ekaggatā-citta* with *nibbāna* as its object." We have already learned that *ekaggatā-citta* is the mind gathered together into one pinnacle, or peak; true *samādhi* has *nibbāna* or *santi* (spiritual tranquility) as its object. So when *pīti* causes complications, disturbances, and difficulties, we chase it away because we do not want or need it. We aim at the one-pinnacled mind that has *santi* or *nibbāna* as its object. The feeling of *pīti* dissolves because we do not want it anymore. This is a skillful means that uses *samādhi* to drive away *pīti*.

## THE WISDOM METHOD

Next is the method that uses *paññā* (wisdom) to diminish the strength of *pīti*, to eradicate the influence of *pīti*, or even of *sukha* if we wish. We use the *paññā* that realizes the true nature (characteristics, qualities, conditions) of all things to understand how *pīti* arises and what will cause it to cease. *Pīti* bubbles up when a satisfying condition is achieved. *Pīti* ceases because of the lack of that satisfying condition, and thus we realize that it is illusory and not real. Once we see wisely in this way, the feeling of being agitated by *pīti* will abate.

Another wisdom method is to contemplate the *assāda* and *ādīnava* of *pīti*. *Assāda* is an element's attractive quality, its charm that deliciously tempts the heart. *Pīti* has an enchanting flavor. *Ādīnava* is an element's unhealthy consequences. The *ādīnava* of *pīti* is the fact that it excites and disturbs, that it drives away tranquility and is the foe of *vipassanā*. Once we realize this, *pīti* dissolves. If we see its arising and ceasing, its charm and unwholesomeness, then it dissolves and disappears. This is how to drive off *pīti* with the *paññā* technique.

We should understand completely the meanings of *assāda* and *ādīnava*. The Pali words are even better than the English translations. *Assāda* is the attractive, satisfying, lovely, infatuating quality or charm of something. *Ādīnava* is the unsound or noxious quality of a thing. There is no excuse for us to be deceived by these two. Once we see them, we will know that being pleased by and falling in love with anything is positive foolishness, and to hate something is negative foolishness. If we know that these two constantly deceive and lure us into loving and hating, then we will learn from them not to indulge in liking and disliking, and we will be freed from the power of objects. For example, money has both *assāda* and *ādīnava*. Once we know these two, money will not mislead us or make us crazy.

The safest thing we can do is to understand this pair fully. Know the *assāda* and *ādīnava* of *pīti* and you will tire of *pīti*. It will flee by itself. This is how to use the wisdom method to chase away *pīti*. Even *sukha* should not be indulged. Although we may save some *sukha* for a beneficial purpose, we do not get lost in it. We should remember *assāda* and *ādīnava* for the rest of our lives. Then they will become the kind of charm or talisman that truly protects rather than endangers.

At this point, the mind is able to regulate the feelings. It has developed the kind of mastery and self-control where the feelings no longer have the power to drag us this way or that. We have discussed the *sukha-vedanā*, the group of pleasant feelings, that pull the mind in an agreeable direction, in a positive way. There is another set of *vedanā* that pull us in a negative way, in an undesirable, unsatisfactory direction. We also need to be aware of these unpleasant feelings, the *dukkha-vedanā*, and how to keep these feelings of displeasure and unhappiness from dragging us into a state of *dukkha*. They can be overcome with the same method as we used on *pīti*. We can control all happy or unhappy feelings. In fact, we become controllers of all feelings without exception. We practice by bringing any *vedanā* into the mind and experiencing it fully. Then we scrutinize it with *paññā* to drive that feeling away. Experience this ability to drive away any kind of *vedanā*. Know that the feelings cannot condition the *citta* anymore. Rehearse this technique with every inhalation and exhalation until you become deft and expert at it. Thus, you will meet with success in the practice of step eight.

## WHY BOTHER?

One last point to consider is why we bother talking so much about the feelings. Why is it necessary to include them in this line of practice? Why not hurry on to *vipassanā* and get to *nibbāna* as fast as possible? The reason is that we must understand the *vedanā* and regulate them to help us control the mind as our practice continues on to the realization of the path, fruitions, and *nibbānas* (*magga-phala-nibbāna*), which is our primary purpose.

We also have a special secondary purpose. That is, once we can regulate the feelings, we will be able to keep our life on the correct path. When we are foolish about the *vedanā*, we become slaves to materialism. This happens when we indulge in material pleasures, that is, the flavors of feelings. All the crises in this world have their origin in people not understanding the *vedanā*, giving in to the *vedanā*, being enamored with the *vedanā*. The feelings entice us to act in ways that lead to disagreements, quarrels, conflicts, and eventually, war. Sometimes they even lead to world wars, all because people act unwisely through the deceptions of *vedanā*.

By now we surely realize that the feelings must be understood. We must know their secrets and learn to regulate them if there is to be peace in this world. There is no need to talk of realizing *nibbāna*, when merely living on this planet in peace with others—or even with ourselves—is more than we can manage right now. It is clearly important that we take advantage of this ability to control the feelings for the rest of our lives. This tetrad has been included in the practice of *ānāpānasati* because of the great power and importance of the *vedanā*.

This is the second tetrad of *ānāpānasati*. It is the foundation for the third tetrad, contemplation of mind, which we will consider next.

# 6

# Contemplating the *Citta*

OUR STUDY OF THE THIRD TETRAD of *ānāpānasati* is concerned with the *citta*, the mind-heart, and is known as *cittānupassanā* (contemplation of *citta*).

Before specifically discussing the third tetrad, there is a very important point that we sometimes forget to stress. Every time you sit down to practice *ānāpānasati*—every sitting and every session— you must begin with step one, experiencing the long breath. It does not matter which step you were doing yesterday, today you must start again at the very beginning. Each session is brand new. From the long breath, move on to the short breath, and so on. Progress from one step to the next, completely fulfilling each step before moving on, until you come to the step where you left off the last time. Each step depends upon the previous one. If you are unable to do the first step, then there is no possibility of going on to further steps. Even now, when we intend to do *cittānupassanā*, we must start at step one. This holds true for all sixteen steps. With every inhalation and exhalation, we practice in this way. Do not forget. We always begin practicing with step one—every time, every session, every step that we practice.

After successfully completing the first two tetrads, we begin to work on the third, *cittānupassanā* (contemplation of mind). The first step of this tetrad is contemplating or experiencing the mind in all its aspects. This is called *citta-paṭisaāvedī* (experiencing the condition or state of the mind during any given moment). Many different states of mind have arisen since the beginning of the practice. We must observe the state of the mind at each step. What is its condition now? How is it changing? What arises in the *citta*? What are the mind's characteristics at this moment? In previous steps, we have emphasized certain things that the mind knows or experiences. Now, we are ready to observe *citta* itself. We must observe until we know directly what the mind is like in this moment. What kind of experience is it? Step nine begins with experiencing the *citta* through each moment of practice.

## DEFILED OR NOT?

There are many different characteristics of the mind to contemplate, but they all must happen naturally by themselves. We observe these characteristics as they really exist, in the very moment of their existence. As it is said in the traditional way of speaking, the characteristics to note begin with "whether the mind has lust (*rāga*) or is free of lust." The meaning of *rāga* is broad. Sexual lust is called *rāga*; lust toward objects such as money, jewelry, gold, food, housing, and possessions is also called *rāga*. There can also be lust toward individuals: for instance, love (nonsexual) of one's employees or servants. The Pali term *rāga* has this wide array of meanings, both sexual and nonsexual. Does the *citta* have any of these types of *rāga* at this moment, or is it free of lust? If there is lust, then thoroughly contemplate its presence to distinguish what kind of lust it is. Know what it is to have *rāga* in the mind. If there is no lust, then contemplate its absence. Breathe in and breathe out while experiencing the actual state of mind in this moment.

The next characteristic of mind to contemplate is *dosa* (anger, hatred, aversion). The meaning of *dosa* is also broad. Sometimes an external object—a person or situation—causes us to be angry. Any dislike in the mind is *dosa*; it can even arise from within, without any external object. When the mind is oppressed, irritated, offended, or resentful, it is called *dosa*. We contemplate whether this mind has *dosa*. If the *citta* is free of anger and hatred, then know that state. This is the second characteristic to observe.

The third characteristic to observe is *moha* (delusion and confusion). *Moha* is feeling infatuated with something because of not knowing that object as it really is. For example, when we are doubtful about something, we cannot help but think about it. Or when there is hope or expectation, we cannot avoid dwelling on it. *Moha* can mean "astray or lost," and it can mean "dark or dim," that is, full of doubt and ignorance. When one kind of thought or another ferments in the mind, it is called *moha*. We should know whether or not there is delusion in the mind. If there is *moha*, then realize it and contemplate it. If the *citta* is empty of delusion, then contemplate its absence. Always contemplate this state of mind while breathing in and breathing out. This is the third characteristic.

There is a simple way of distinguishing among these three states: *rāga*, *dosa*, and *moha*. If there is any feeling of wanting, that is, wanting to gather toward, to pull in, to hug and to hold, such a feeling is *rāga*. It has a most positive character. The second, *dosa*, does not like, does not want. It has a negative character. *Dosa* pushes away, knocks away, even to the extent of wanting to kill. *Rāga* pulls in and *dosa* pushes away. The third, *moha*, is ignorant. It does not know what is wrong and right, good and evil, according to reality. It is running around in circles. This is how the three differ. One gathers in, one pushes away, and one runs in circles. We should be able to observe the differences and to call them by their correct names. We know *rāga*, *dosa*, and *moha* by observing their activities of pulling in, pushing away, and running in circles.

Next, we need to know whether the mind is distracted or undistracted. The distracted mind lacks one-pointedness; it is unable to rest and relax and has no stillness or calm. Further, distraction annoys us. Is the *citta* distracted? Or is it free of distraction, in a state of normality? We contemplate the mind's character while breathing in and breathing out. We practice in order to know all types of *citta*.

## COMMON OR EXALTED?

Next, we observe whether there is a superior state of mind, one better than usual, or merely a common state. In Pali, the superior state is called *mahaggatā*. In ordinary language we would say there is an awareness that is sharper than usual, more satisfying than usual, higher than usual. Does our *citta* have such an awareness now? If so, contemplate it. If not, know that a common state of mind exists at this moment. Contemplate this pair while breathing in and breathing out.

Another pair of states to consider is whether or not this mind is supreme and unsurpassed. That is, has our *citta* achieved that most advanced state where there is nothing better? Or has our mind not yet reached the most advanced state so that there are finer things yet to come? This one is difficult to know because the supreme, most developed state of mind is the *citta* of an *arahant* ("worthy one," fully awakened, perfected human being). If we are not yet *arahants*, common sense tells us whether we have the type of *citta* that is most satisfying or whether there is still something more to be developed. Do we feel that we have achieved final satisfaction? Or do we feel that there should be something even more satisfying than this? This pair is about the *citta* having or not having something superior to it. If there is this highest mind, contemplate it clearly in order to understand it. Breathe in and breathe out with this kind of awareness.

The next pair is whether or not the mind is concentrated. Is it or is it not in *samādhi*? Concentrate the *citta*. Even if the mind is not in full *samādhi* right now, the influence of *samādhi* will probably keep it concentrated. This too can be called a concentrated mind. Know whether the mind is concentrated or not while breathing in and breathing out.

The last pair is to see if the mind has been liberated, if it is empty of attachment (*upādāna*), not grasping or clinging to anything, or if it is not yet liberated and still clinging to something. Does the mind have attachment or not? This is what we mean by asking whether or not the *citta* is liberated. Right now, is there anything arresting the mind or is it free? Whatever the case, know it clearly. Breathe in and out with this awareness. Make it as distinct as possible.

## KNOWING OURSELVES

By practicing like this, we learn to know ourselves and the kinds of thoughts that are typical for us. Then we understand ourselves well. What kinds of *citta* are habitual in us? Generally, the mind's thoughts tend to follow some object. By observing these tendencies, we know ourselves better. This is a special benefit of this step. Our primary aim, however, is to know our mind as completely as possible. Thoroughly understanding our own *citta* is the specific objective of this step. This is how to practice step one of the third tetrad, that is, step nine overall.

## DELIGHTING THE MIND

Step two of this tetrad is delighting the mind (*abhippamodayaā cittaā*). From the beginning, we have been training in various ways of controlling the mind. In the second tetrad, we developed the mind's ability to be independent of feeling and to have control over the *vedanā*. This means the mind is under control.[8] Once we fully know the various mental states and conditions, both positive and negative, then we can put the *citta* into any state that is appropriate or desirable. Step ten is to make the mind joyful, delighted, and content. It is important to be able to control the mind so that it feels satisfied and glad while breathing in and out.

When the mind is sad, sorrowful, or without joy, we can let go of the sorrow and bring the mind into a joyful state. Or even when the mind is in a normal state, we can always gladden or delight it by using this technique. This is very useful. We do not have to endure a sorrowful mind because we can control it. Whenever needed, we can have the energy to do whatever work is required. We can be joyful at any time. But be careful—the words *joyfulness* and *delight* have two types of meaning. There is the ordinary, worldly kind of delight that is rooted in materialism and sensuality. Although this is one kind of joy, it is not the specific kind of joy we are interested in. We require the delight that comes with knowing and using Dhamma. We need not depend on material or sensual stimulants, for we have Dhamma to help delight the *citta*. Thus, there are two kinds of joyfulness: defiled joyfulness and joyfulness free of defilement (*kilesa*). Both kinds of joy are available to us. If you want defiled joyfulness, it is very easy to obtain. The delight derived from Dhamma, however, must be achieved correctly. For this reason, we ought to examine it more closely.

## DELIGHTED BY DHAMMA

It is easy to delight the mind when we understand the cause of joyfulness. Joyfulness comes from the feeling of being successful, of having correctly and successfully completed an activity. An easy way to delight the mind is to return to practicing steps one, two, and three again. Go back to the beginning and practice each step successfully. Then there will be contentment and joyfulness with each completed step. This kind of gladness is associated with Dhamma. We return to practicing step one again, but now we focus specifically upon the feeling of success, contentment, and joyful delight. Proceed through each of the steps in the same way until you arrive at the feeling of joyfulness that satisfies us the most. Joyfulness comes from contentment, and contentment comes from achieving success in some activity. By being certain that we are safe and liberated from bondage, we will experience contentment and joyfulness.

An easy method is to reflect upon achieving what is good. We have obtained the good life, a life that has discovered the Dhamma and is certain to eradicate *dukkha*. We are the most fortunate of human beings, one who has found Dhamma and is able to eliminate *dukkha*. By reflecting in this way, we are joyful and happy. This is the way to be exceedingly glad and delighted. Obtaining what is good, achieving the good life, being a good human being, discovering enough Dhamma to ensure that we will not suffer—this kind of reflection is a simple way for the *citta* to experience joy.

When we are certain that we can extinguish *dukkha*, or when we have gained the best that humans can possibly achieve, then it is normal for us to be joyful and content. We study the Dhamma to understand what will eradicate suffering, to realize our maximum human potential. Then we are content. We are able to delight and gladden the *citta* using this skillful technique.

## CONCENTRATING THE MIND

Once we are able to delight the mind as we wish, we train in the next step. The objective of step eleven is to concentrate the mind (*samādahaā citta*). This step is not difficult because we have been practicing with concentration from the beginning, especially in step four (calming the body-conditioner) and step eight (calming the mind-conditioner). If we could do it before, then we can do it now. So we concentrate the mind in *samādhi* and immediately drive away any unwanted feelings. Then the *citta* is concentrated and happy and is skillfully able to perform various duties. This ability is most advantageous.

This brings us to a common problem. Most people misunderstand, thinking that if the mind is in *samādhi*, we must sit absolutely still—stiff and unable to move. Or they think that in *samādhi* we should experience no sensation whatsoever. This is wrong understanding. To sit still and stiff like a log is only a training exercise in higher levels of *samādhi*. Developing the deeper concentrations of the second, third, and fourth *jhāna*, up to the point where the body does not breathe, are just training exercises. Nevertheless, if the mind is able to develop these very high levels of concentration, it should have no problems with the lower levels. Here in step eleven, concentrating the mind means to train the mind so that it has good qualities and is ready for work. It is prepared to perform its duties as needed. From the previous step the *citta* knows how to be happy. When it is happy, the *citta* is highly capable of performing its functions. We should not misunderstand and think that when the mind is in *samādhi*, we must be rigid like a rock or a log.

## STABILITY, PURITY, ACTIVENESS

If the mind has correct *samādhi*, we will observe in the mind three distinct qualities. The quality of mind that is firm, steady, undistracted, and focused on a single object is called *samāhito* (stability, collectedness). That mind is clear and pure, not disturbed by anything, unobscured by defilement. A mind empty of defilement is called *parisuddho* (purity). Such a *citta* is fit and supremely prepared to perform the duties of the mind. This is called *kammanīyo* (activeness, readiness). It might be wise to memorize these three words: *samāhito* (stability), *parisuddho* (purity), and *kammanīyo* (activeness). For correct concentration all three of these qualities must be present. This kind of concentration can be used not only in formal meditation practice but in any of the necessary activities of life.

These three qualities can be present while walking, standing, sitting, or lying down. There is an interesting passage in a Pali text; it states that if these three qualities are present while standing, that is called "divine standing." If these three qualities are present while walking, then that is "divine walking." If all three are present while sitting, that is "divine sitting." If these qualities are present while lying down, then it is "divine lying down." Obviously, concentration is more than sitting like a lump of rock or a block of wood—stiff, rigid, and dead to the world. Instead, with concentration the *citta* is perfectly ready to perform its duty, namely, to grow in knowledge and understanding from moment to moment. At the very least, the *citta* will be happy when these three qualities are present, and being happy is also a duty of the *citta*.

The practitioner whose mind is concentrated with these three qualities is known as "one who has a concentrated mind." The Pali word is *samāhito* (one who is concentrated). In Pali, Lord Buddha is quoted as saying, "When the mind is concentrated, it knows all *dhammas* as they truly are" (*samāhito yathābhutaā pajānāti*). This is the supreme benefit of *samāhito*: the *citta* is concentrated on knowing all things as they really are. If there are any problems in life that we cannot answer, then concentrate the mind and the answers will automatically come. Wherever it goes, the concentrated mind sees things according to reality. If we look within ourselves, we see all things according to truth. This means that if the *citta* is accompanied by the three qualities of *samāhito,* we will easily see *aniccaā, dukkhaā,* and *anattā.*

We can observe that these three qualities are interdependent; they are interconnected in a single unity. There cannot be purity of mind without stability of mind. If there is no purity, there is also no stability. And there must be stability and purity for there to be activeness. The three work together as the three factors of the concentrated mind. Moreover, the three must be equal and unified to be called *samāhito.* Then they become extremely beneficial, valuable, and powerful. This kind of concentration is able to solve the questions of life, including both the natural problems of this material world and the questions of a "supernatural" order above the world.

Finally, we must understand this essential point: when the mind is in *samādhi,* we can walk or stand or sit or lie down or work or taste the fruit of our labor or help others or help ourselves. The *samādhi-citta* can be used on any problem, in any situation. It can be used to solve all problems. Be interested in this word *samāhito*— one who has *samādhi* and is able to perform every kind of duty.

## LIBERATING THE MIND

While breathing in and breathing out, we practice until we are capable of having the mind of *samāhito* with three qualities. We have then completed step eleven. We now come to step twelve, which is liberating the mind (*vimocayaā-citta*). Liberating the mind means not letting the mind become attached to anything. We make the mind let go of anything it is grasping. Such a mind is spotlessly clean; it is free. Liberating the mind from all attachments has two aspects: the mind can let go of all these things, or we can take these things away from the mind. The results are the same. We take away all the things that the *citta* should not hold on to. Then we observe if there is anything to which the *citta* continues to cling. If so, we try to release those things from the mind. This is step twelve.

It is essential that we thoroughly understand what is called "attachment." Although it is a mental phenomenon, we use words from the physical-mental realm to discuss it. We use words like *cling, grasp,* and *be attached.* Yet, it is a mental activity. The mind is ignorant and acts out of ignorance. Thus, it causes the activity we call clinging or grasping or being attached. We ought to study this carefully, for it is something that exists in all people, in everyone's daily life. Briefly, attachment is to regard something as "I" or "mine." If we understand attachment, then the practice of this step will go smoothly.

The most direct way to practice step twelve is to examine the danger, the pain, and the suffering present in any moment that we cling to something as "I" or "mine." Scrutinize the dangerous and painful consequences that all attachment inevitably brings. Then examine and realize the benefits and advantages of non-attachment. When we are not attached, what benefits do we receive? What kind of happiness is present? Observe carefully. When we grasp onto something, what type and degree of pain and suffering results? Examine both sides of the coin. Contemplate the suffering of attachment and the value of non-attachment as they continuously alternate in the mind. Through this kind of contemplation the mind is automatically liberated. The mind will naturally let go of things, and things will naturally let go of the mind through observing these two facts. Observe until you see the penalty and lowliness of attachment. Observe until you see the advantages of non-attachment. Observe this every time you breathe in and out. This is how to practice this step.

## FOUR KINDS OF ATTACHMENT

The objects of attachment are numerous. Furthermore, they are subtle and profound. By this we mean that they are difficult to see, hear, and understand. Nevertheless, we can identify four types, or modes, of attachment. The first category is all the material objects valued by sensuality (*kāma*), such as possessions, necessities, gems, jewelry, gold, and money; or in other words, the things we see, hear, smell, taste, feel, and think about. All these are the foundations of sensuality and sexuality. These are objects of attachment to sexuality.

The other three categories are immaterial objects of attachment. The second category consists of our incorrect opinions, beliefs, views, and theories. These are the things that we cannot understand, that we cannot possibly know, but because of *avijjā* (ignorance) we accept and are attached to them. We have many such incorrect opinions and views.

The third category includes the traditional activities and practices that we follow. All of them, both the religious and the secular, are superstitious. There are many of these customs with which we identify.

Last and most important of all is the category of all the things that we are attached to as "I" or "mine." These four main categories of attachment include all the things that we grasp. Observe them and see the pain and suffering of clinging to them. See the value of not clinging to them. Continually examine every kind of attachment with every inhalation and exhalation. In this way they are released in an automatic letting go. Release the objects of attachment. Let go, let go, let go.

When we look at Christianity, we see that it shares this concern about attachment. In fact, the primary symbol of Christianity—the cross—teaches the "I" (the upright) and the cutting of the "I" (the cross-member). This symbolizes getting rid of attachment. All religions agree on their major goal: the eradication of attachment to "I" and "mine." This is the highest, most sublime practice. It removes those fundamental difficulties—selfishness in particular—that are the source of all other problems. Cut out selfishness and problems end. We should become interested in letting go of all things. Letting go of the four types of attachment is the best thing we can do.

The mind must also let go of the things that are disturbing the *citta* right at this moment, such as the *nivaraṭa* (hindrances). These are moods that arise in the mind out of habit and tendencies of thought. The five *nivarata* are feelings of sensuality, aversion, depression and drowsiness, agitation and distraction, and doubt and uncertainty. We must drive away these five *nivarata*. Furthermore, the *kilesa* (defilements)—the emotions of *lobha* (greed), *dosa* (anger), and *moha* (delusion)—must go. Any feelings of liking and disliking, any moods of satisfaction and dissatisfaction, any attachments to dualistic things must be removed. Eventually, we will realize that no problems remain that will put the *citta* into *dukkha*. If there is attachment, there is *dukkha*. When the mind is empty of attachment, it experiences no *dukkha* because there is no foundation for *dukkha*.

Whenever the mind sees something clinging to it, it releases that object. Practicing like this every time we breathe in and breathe out is step twelve, the last step of the third tetrad. Altogether there are four steps that deal exclusively with the *citta*: experiencing the different states of mind, gladdening the mind, concentrating the mind, and liberating the mind. Through them we successfully complete our study of the mind.

So far, we have discussed three of the four tetrads. The next chapter concerns the remaining tetrad, the most important of all.

# 7

# The Supreme

IN THIS CHAPTER, we will discuss the fourth tetrad, the final four steps of *ānāpānasati*. In this tetrad we specifically study and examine Dhamma, or truth. You will recall that the first tetrad concerned the breath and the body. The second tetrad dealt with those feelings that result from the calming of the body-conditioner, the breathing. We studied the mind's feelings although not yet the mind (*citta*) itself. We studied the mind-conditioners and learned about the conditioning of the *citta*. Then we learned to control the *citta-sankhāra*, the mind-conditioners. In the third tetrad we studied the *citta* and practiced various ways of controlling the mind. Now that this well-trained mind has been brought under control, in the fourth tetrad we use it to study Dhamma, the truth of nature. Please observe how the four tetrads are interconnected: first, the *kāya-sankhāra*; second, the *citta-sankhāra*; third the *citta* itself; and finally Dhamma, the facts (*saccadhamma*) of nature (*dhamma-jāti*).

The reasoning here is simple. Once the mind is under our power and within our control, we put this mind to work. The mind has a great deal of *kammanīyo*, readiness or activeness, from the practice of concentrating the mind in the third tetrad. The mind is fit and ready to do its duties. In Pali another word is used in this context—*mudu* (gentle). Whereas before the *citta* was hard and stiff, now it is gentle and supple. The mind is very sensitive and quick, in a condition that is ready to be used. Consequently, we use the mind to do the work of the fourth tetrad, where the first duty is to contemplate impermanence.

## THE IMPERMANENCE OF *ĀNĀPĀNASATI*

From the beginning, a fundamental principle of this entire practice has been to use elements already existing within us as the objects of our study and practice. We prefer not to use external objects. Once we completely understand the internals, we can extrapolate to the externals. We should not forget this important principle: we must examine things that exist internally. Therefore, for this step of *aniccānupassī* (contemplating impermanence), we return to the beginning step. First, we contemplate just the breath until we see that it is impermanent. We observe that the breath changes and becomes long. Its long duration is impermanent, always changing, getting longer or shorter. Its shortness is impermanent as well. The various conditions and characteristics of the breath are impermanent. The breath's effect on the body is also impermanent.

Next, observe that both bodies—the breath-body and the flesh-body—are impermanent. Then, watch the calming of the breath; here, impermanence becomes even more obvious. The breath changes from coarse to calm, but even that calmness is impermanent. The state of the breath keeps changing. Contemplate each step, one at a time, until each phase is seen to be impermanent.

Eventually, the feelings of *pīti* and *sukha* arise. Watch them one by one. See impermanence in each and every aspect of these *vedanā*. Contemplate the impermanence of the conditioning of the mind by the feelings. The calming of these feelings is impermanent as well.

Next, we watch the *citta* itself; it, too, is impermanent. The gladdening and refreshing of the mind as it changes to delight and joyfulness is impermanent. Contemplate the impermanence of this freshness and delight along with its various conditions and flavors. Concentration itself is impermanent for it changes to non-concentration. The activeness of *samādhi* is impermanent. Impermanence manifests right there in that activeness. Even the liberating of the mind is only a temporary liberation here and thus is also impermanent.

Realize impermanence in each and every step, in each and every one of the interconnected points, phases, and aspects of this practice. Directly experience impermanence in everything. Redo each of the steps. Make the impermanence of each step absolutely clear, undoubtedly obvious, completely certain. This is how we contemplate the impermanence of all these passing phenomena, which are collectively known as *sankhāra*. In step thirteen, we contemplate the impermanence of the *sankhāra* (conditioned things, concoctions).

## MORE TO IT THAN JUST IMPERMANENCE

Now, observe that in the realization of impermanence there is the simultaneous realization of many other aspects. When impermanence is truly seen, it also has the characteristic of *dukkham*, namely, it is painful and unbearable. We can also find the characteristic of not-self (*anattā*) in it. As these things are always changing, impermanent, unsatisfactory, and beyond our control, we realize *anattā* as well. Then we see that they are void of selfhood, which is *suññatā*. We see that they are just thus, just like that. Impermanence is just thus, just like that, thusness. And so, *tathatā* is seen as well.

Please understand that the realizations of these truths are interrelated. From seeing impermanence, we see unsatisfactoriness, see *anattā*, see *suññatā*, see *tathatā*, and see *idappaccayatā* (conditionality, the law of cause and effect) as well. Each continues into the next. A complete realization of impermanence must include unsatisfactoriness, not-self, voidness, thusness, and the law of causality. When we see all of these, then we have seen impermanence completely and in the most profound way. This is how we fully realize the impermanence of the *sankhāra*.

We have already explained *sankhāra* and practiced it in lessons three and seven.[9] Remember that there are three meanings to this word: the conditions that are concocted, the concocters that condition other things, and the activity of conditioning or concocting. Various causes, conditions, and ingredients must be concocted and compounded in order to use the term *sankhāra*. The characteristic of conditioners is impermanence. The characteristic of things conditioned is impermanence. The characteristic of the activity or process of conditioning is impermanence. To see all three aspects like this is to realize impermanence in the most profound and complete way.

Merely seeing *aniccam* by itself, rather than seeing it completely in all of its characteristics, is nothing extraordinary. To be complete, the realization must encompass *dukkham*, *anattā*, *suññatā*, *tathatā*, and *idappaccayatā*. To see *aniccam* alone, in an incomplete way that does not include *dukkham* and *anattā*, is neither profound nor sufficient to solve our problems. Thus, "realizing *aniccam*" in this context must encompass a realization as deep as *dukkham*, *anattā*, *suññatā*, *tathatā*, and *idappaccayatā*.

This is illustrated in the following story. In *The Basket of Discourses* (*suttanta-piṭaka*) of the Pali Canon, the Buddha mentioned that there was a religious teacher at that time named Araka who taught about impermanence as often as the Buddha did, but went no further and said nothing about *dukkhaṁ* and *anattā*. This is interesting because at the time of the Buddha there lived the Greek philosopher Heraclitus. The Buddha said that Araka lived in a distant land where he taught about impermanence or flux. The Blessed One was probably referring to Heraclitus, whose central teaching was *panta rhei* (Greek, "everything flows" or "all is flux"). Heraclitus taught only impermanence, however, and was unable to extend this insight to include *dukkhaṁ, anattā, suññatā, tathatā,* and *idappaccayatā*. Thus, it was not a successful teaching. Otherwise, another buddha would have arisen right then and there. Knowledge about impermanence was well spread both within India and abroad. "Distant land" probably meant a foreign country; thus we might suppose that Araka and Heraclitus were the same person.

The essential point is that seeing *aniccaṁ* alone is not enough. We must see *aniccaṁ* such that it shines onto *dukkhaṁ, anattā, suññatā, tathatā,* and *idappaccayatā*—the entire string of realization. The short phrase *aniccānupassī* (contemplating impermanence) includes the realization of unsatisfactoriness, not-self, voidness, thusness, and conditionality as well.

### DISSOLVING ATTACHMENT

Now, observe—study closely until you see it—that the realization of *aniccaṁ* dissolves *upādāna*, dissolves attachment. This is crucial. Realizing *aniccaṁ* dissolves attachment because we realize the pain and suffering of that attachment. *Upādāna* dissolves until less and less remains. Such is the result of realizing impermanence. It makes us weary, bored, and disenchanted with all the things to which we continue to be attached and were ever attached. Then *upādāna* begins to dissolve. This is the result of truly seeing impermanence.

The second step of this tetrad, or step fourteen overall, is contemplating fading away (*virāgānupassī*). We already began to observe this in step thirteen when the contemplation of impermanence led to the dissolving of attachment. Now we focus upon and study dissolving, or *virāga*. *Vi*, in this case, means "not" or "not having." *Rāga* is another name for attachment. Thus, *virāga* means "without attachment." Watching attachment dissolve is like watching the stains in a cloth slowly fade away, bleached out by sunlight, until the cloth is white. This is a material analogy of *virāga* that helps to explain the mental fading away of attachment. *Upādāna* dissolves under the light of seeing things as they truly are—*aniccaṁ*, *dukkhaṁ*, *anattā*, *suññatā*, *tathatā*, and *idappaccayatā*. We know that attachment is lessening when we are even-minded toward *sankhāra*, namely, toward all things to which we were once attached. When we are unprejudiced toward them all, we realize *virāga*, the fading away of attachment. Contemplate this with every inhalation and exhalation. This is how to practice step fourteen.

The result of this fading away of attachment is the even-minded stillness of non-attachment. We can observe this quite easily, for example, as our erotic love for things to which we were once attached begins to fade. Anger toward past, or even present, objects of our displeasure dissolves away. We are no longer afraid of the things we once feared. We are gradually less and less afraid until fear disappears. The same is true for hatred, envy, jealousy, worry, anxiety, longing after the past, and so on. Each of these indicators lessens and shrinks until the mind is able to keep still and silent. The phrase "keep still and silent" means simply not to grasp, cling, or regard anything as "I" or "mine." Contemplate impermanence until the attachment dissolves, until we can remain still, silent, and even-minded. This is how to practice this step.

### QUENCHING *DUKKHA*

Step fifteen, *nirodhānupassī*, is the study and contemplation of the quenching of attachment. We observe the cessation of attachment, the nonexistence of attachment, while breathing in and breathing out. We can observe quenching or cessation from a variety of perspectives: the quenching of attachment to "self"; the quenching of selfishness; the quenching of greed, anger, and delusion; and the quenching of all experiences of *dukkha*. All occur with the quenching of attachment. There are many forms of *nirodha*.

When we speak of quenching, remember that the ending of

*dukkha* is what the practice of Dhamma is all about. Here, we observe different aspects of *dukkha* to see how they are quenched. The first aspect is the ending of fearfulness, the horror of birth, aging, illness, and death. Aging, illness, and death will never again terrify our mind. This is one type of quenching. The next aspect is the cessation of the various symptoms or conditions of *dukkha*, such as sorrow, grief, lamentation, despair, sadness, pain, frustration, and depression. All of these symptoms of *dukkha* are quenched. The third aspect is related to our hopes and wants, to attractive and unattractive things. Experiencing things we do not like is *dukkha*. Being separated from the things we like is *dukkha*. Not getting what we want is *dukkha*. These aspects of *dukkha* are quenched as well.

Lastly, clinging to one of the five *khandha* (groups, aggregates, clusters), grasping the five groups (*pañca-khandha*), as "self" or "belonging to self," as "I" or "mine" is *dukkha*. These five groups of things to which the mind habitually is attached are body, feeling, perception, thought, and sense-consciousness. These are the summation of all *dukkha*, the burdens of life. A full realization of this step must include all four aspects of *dukkha's* quenching. Quench the fear of birth, aging, illness, and death. Quench the symptoms of *dukkha*, such as pain, sorrow, sadness, and despair. Quench the wants and desires of agreeable and disagreeable things. Finally, quench the view of any of the five *khandha* as "self." When these four aspects are quenched, then *dukkha* is quenched. We should not underestimate this important realization.

Thus, we realize the voidness or nonexistence of attachment through the quenching, disappearing, and ending of attachment. We experience the absence of attachment, in any of the aspects mentioned above, while we breathe in and breathe out. Or more simply, we drink, taste, and savor the flavor of *nibbāna*. *Nirodha* and *nibbāna* are synonyms; we can use them interchangeably. Thus, to contemplate the quenching of attachment is to contemplate *nibbāna*.

### THROWING IT ALL BACK

The last step, the fourth step of the fourth tetrad, the sixteenth step of *ānāpānasati* is called *patinissaggānupassī* (contemplating throwing back). *Patinissaggā* is a curious word; it means to throw back or give back. When we arrive at this step, we contemplate our throwing back, our returning, everything to which we were once attached. This is step sixteen.

There is a simple metaphor for explaining this step. Throughout our lives we have been thieves. All along, we have been stealing things that exist naturally, that belong to nature, namely, the *sankhāra*. We have plundered them and taken them to be our selves and our possessions. We are nothing but thieves. For this we are being punished by *dukkha*. We suffer *dukkha* because of all our attachment and thieving. As soon as we observe the way things really are through the succession of steps in this tetrad, we let go. We cease being thieves. We return everything to its original owner—nature. It all belongs to nature. Don't claim anything to be "I" or "mine" ever again! Our goal is made clear by this metaphor.

## DROPPING THE BURDENS OF LIFE

The following example illustrates a similar point. In the past we went around foolishly picking up heavy objects, such as boulders.[10] We lugged them along wherever we went. For this we constantly suffered *dukkha*. How many years has this gone on? Now, however, we realize how unwise we were in creating such problems for ourselves. We realize how burdensome these boulders are, and we just toss them away. Without these burdens we are light; all our problems disappear. Before, life itself seemed to be a burden because of our stupidity. We clung to those natural *sankhāra*, carried them everywhere, and thus weighed ourselves down terribly. Now we throw them off. This is another metaphor that describes the final step of *ānāpānasati*.

The practice of this last step is to train in throwing away the burdens of life. Throw them away until no burdens remain. Before, we lived under their weight; their heaviness oppressed us. This is called "living beneath the world" or "drowning in the world." Once we can toss away the burdens that hold us down, that trap us beneath the world, we ascend. We are above the world. We are "lords of the world." This is the true meaning of freedom and well-being.

You should remember the meanings of these two conditions.

"Living beneath the world" is *lokiya*. "Living above the world" is *lokuttara*. During the practice of step sixteen every problem related to these two meanings will be solved. Let us understand clearly and perfectly that whenever we are foolish, we pick up weights and pile them up as burdens of life. Once we know what they are doing to us, we throw them off. Now we no longer have any burdens. Living under the world and living above the world are totally different. Whoever wants to be free, to be at ease, to be above the world, ought to try their best to practice according to this truth as much as possible—starting right now.

### THE SUPREME EMANCIPATION

Be well aware that this is the way to emancipation. *Ānāpānasati* successfully practiced through this final step brings emancipation, or liberation. When we are liberated from all bonds, we either let go of all burdens or release ourselves out from under those burdens. Whether we say "letting go of ourselves" or "letting go of the burdens," the meaning of the realization is the same. There is "letting go," and the result is emancipation. Or it might be called "salvation," "deliverance," "release," or "liberation." They all signify that we have obtained the best thing possible for human beings. We have not wasted our lives and the opportunity of having found the Dhamma, which is the best thing that human beings can obtain. This is the end of the story.

We have completed a thorough discussion of all the lessons and tetrads of *ānāpānasati* as taught by the Lord Buddha. You should now have a good understanding of the entire process as well as of the individual steps. Before finishing our discussion, let's consider the wonderful fruits and benefits of practicing *ānāpānasati*.

# 8

# The Highest Benefits

IN THIS CHAPTER, we will summarize all of the inquiries into *ānāpānasati* covered by the previous chapters. We will summarize the sixteen steps in terms of their essential characteristics, their value and benefits, and the means of realizing those benefits. We shall examine these benefits carefully, so that we will be able to make full use of them according to their meaning.

Let us not forget that we are talking about nature, about four aspects of nature, and the law of nature manifest in these four aspects: *kāya, vedanā, citta,* and Dhamma. These are nature, pure and simple. So we should understand *dhamma-jāti* (see chapter 1). *Dhamma-jāti* both *is* the law of nature and *follows* the law of nature; nature and its law can never be separated. As living creatures, our duty is to understand and use nature for our highest benefit. Although we cannot control it, we can use it to our advantage when we act correctly according to its law. We know these four natures for the benefit of our life, however long it may last.

## *KĀYA*: COOLING EMOTIONS

The first subject in the practice of mindfulness with breathing is the *kāya* (the body, bodies). We can understand without explanation the body's importance in life. It is the foundation for the mind. We require a *kāya* that is ready and able to maintain and support itself, as well as the mind, in ways beneficial for life. Further, we need to understand how to control this *kāya* according to our needs through the technique of regulating the breath. There are many advantages in knowing how to regulate the breath. First, we can change our moods and emotions. For example, when we are angry, we can quickly let go of that anger by breathing long. By breathing deep and long, the anger will disappear. When we are worried and unable to think straight, we breathe longer and longer to force away that worry. Or we can also change from one train of thought to another by breathing long, which will wipe out the unwanted thoughts or emotions and replace them with something more orderly and normal. Through this practice, we are able to think what needs to be thought. We can see that there is more to *kāya* than just the flesh-body; it carries over to the *citta* as well.

The breath alone is well worth knowing, even if only in terms of health. If we know how to breathe properly, we will have good health. Thus, the body and everything associated with the body—the breath, the emotions, our health—is considered to be a very important subject. It is hoped that you will be able to get the fullest benefits from this stage of *ānāpānasati*.

## *VEDANĀ*: STOPPING THE SPINNING

The feelings are the second item. If you are unaware of the feelings, you might think they are unimportant. In reality, they are of the greatest importance to human beings in that they spin us around at their will. Furthermore, they also spin the whole world around. Whatever feelings we desire—and everyone craves them—incite us to all kinds of behavior. Everyone chases after pleasant feelings and runs away from unpleasant feelings. This is how the *vedanā* keep the whole world spinning. The feelings in people are the causes of all the new, strange inventions and creations that humanity constantly produces. Art, culture, and technology were discovered and produced for the sake of the feelings, which have such great power to force us to follow them. *Vedanā* causes desire. Want is born out of feeling and follows feeling. Consequently, we act according to our desires, causing all manner of occurrences to happen. Even our search for money is a response to *vedanā*, whether because of sensuality and sex or merely because of the ordinary feeling of wishing to be at ease.

We should get to know the things that dominate humanity. The *vedanā* have tremendous power and influence over us. If we cannot control the feelings, we will rise and fall at their whim. This is *dukkha*. We will act out of *vedanā*, which are trapped in ignorance (*avijjā*) and, thus, are incorrect. Animals, too, are directed and compelled by feelings. All their activities are merely searching, hunting, and chasing after the desired *vedanā*. Likewise, people search and hunt for the feelings they want.

Even when you do a meditation retreat, you are hoping to find something that will produce the *vedanā* that please you. Is it not true that in so doing you hope to experience pleasant feelings, such as those that arise from the peace and quiet of a monastery or the joy of meditation? Or that you are trying to get away from some of the agitation, conflict, sorrow, and suffering in the world? These *vedanā* cause all kinds of activity and searching; they compel every kind of effort and endeavor. In effect, they are the masters or dictators of our lives in the most profound way. When we can control them, they do us no harm. When we are unable to control them, we become their slaves. What a pitiful state it is to be a slave to *vedanā*!

There are two kinds of *vedanā*: foolish feelings conditioned by *avijjā* (ignorance) and wise feelings conditioned by *vijjā* (correct knowledge). If we are foolish at the moment of *phassa* (sensory contact), foolish feelings arise. If we are clever and knowledgeable at the moment of *phassa*, wise feelings arise. Foolish feelings lead to ignorant desire, or *taṇhā* (craving). Wise feelings lead to correct desire, to wanting what we ought to want in the right way, that is, to wise wanting. We should make sure that the *vedanā* are always wise feelings. Foolish feelings cause *taṇhā*, or craving, which in turn drags us along behind foolish desires; it also makes us chase after unintelligent needs. Craving can turn wise wants and needs into stupid desires. Foolish *taṇhā* leads us around and around the world, yet we still put up with it. Sometimes we even want to go to the moon! As long as craving remains, there will be no end to it all: endless comings and goings, endless inventions and concoctions, endless desires for the luxurious life. Hence, the benefits of controlling the *vedanā* are enormous. Do not allow them to stir up foolish desires and wants. Let us be interested in the *vedanā* from this perspective.

## *CITTA*: WORKING CORRECTLY

Now we come to the *citta*. Our studies have clearly shown the significance of the *citta* (mind-heart). On the other hand, like the *kāya* and *vedanā*, if the *citta* is established or exists in the wrong way, problems will arise and *dukkha* will occur.

We must understand that we apply three different names to the mind depending on the function that it performs. When it thinks, we call the mind *citta*. When it is aware, feeling, experiencing, and knowing, we call the mind *mano*. And we call the basic function of being conscious at the sense doors in order to see, hear, smell, taste, touch, and think *viññāna*. We focus on the function that the mind performs and name it accordingly; in the case of thinking we name it *citta*, in the case of knowing we name it *mano*, and in the case of basic sensory consciousness we name it *viññāna*.

When the *citta* performs correctly, there are good results, but in order to work correctly the *citta* must be under control. If we do not control it, it will not be correct. When it is not correct, it is said that "nothing will be left in the world." By this we mean that the world exists because we have *citta*; if we did not have *citta*, it would be as if there was no world. If we keep the mind under control and dwelling in correctness, we will receive the fruits of calmness, quiet, and peace. Thoroughly understanding the *citta* to keep it under control is the highest knowledge for human beings to have. We must be especially interested in this.

## DHAMMA: TWO BASIC FACTS

Lastly, we come to Dhamma, or truth. In all things—both those that make up "me" and those that are connected with "me"—there is truth that must be known. If we do not know such truth, or understand it incorrectly, our involvement with life is incorrect. This causes problems and leads to *dukkha*. Such knowledge can be summarized in two areas: that which is compounded (*sankhāra*, concoctions), that is, those things that have causes and conditions, and their opposite, that which is non-compounded. These subjects can be studied through the metaphysical terms "phenomenal" and "noumenal." Noumenal is the opposite of phenomenal; in principle, they are a pair. If something is phenomenal, it is compounded and must exhibit the truth of impermanence (*aniccaṁ*). If something is noumenal, it is non-compounded and is not *aniccaṁ* but *niccaṁ* (permanent). Therefore, we study the *aniccaṁ* of all things until we know well the truth of impermanence. Then we do not become attached to anything. The mind that is not attached to anything will proceed to realize that which is permanent (*niccaṁ*), which is beyond impermanence, namely, the noumenon: *nibbāna*. Under-

standing these two realities—the conditioned and the unconditioned—is of the utmost importance. It is the most important principle of all. The practice of the Dhamma tetrad of *ānāpānasati* leads
to knowing these two realities.

This is the essence of our study within these four areas, and the
knowledge and benefits such study brings. That is the essence of
*ānāpānasati*.

### THE FOUR COMRADE DHAMMAS

There are further benefits from practicing *ānāpānasati*. Through the
practice of *ānāpānasati* we also obtain what are called the "four comrade *dhammas*." The four comrade *dhammas* are *sati, paññā, sampa-
jaññā*, and *samādhi*. While we are living in this world, the four
comrade *dhammas* enable us to subdue all threats; with them we can
rid ourselves of *dukkha*. We must use these four comrades to live,
whether inside or outside the monastery, in family life, or wherever
we find ourselves.

First, we have *sati* (mindfulness, reflective awareness). When a
sense object makes contact, *sati* is there and brings *paññā* (wisdom)
to the experience. Once it arrives, *paññā* transforms into *sampajaññā*
(wisdom-in-action), the specific application of wisdom required by
the situation. Then, *samādhi's* power and strength are added to
*sampa-jaññā*. With all four comrades we are able to conquer every
kind of object that comes in through the eyes, ears, nose, tongue,
body, and mind. The four comrade *dhammas* are unsurpassed
guardians. They watch over and protect us as God is said to do. If
we correctly practice *ānāpānasati*, we will acquire the four comrade
*dhammas*.

### PRACTICING FUNDAMENTAL TRUTHS

Another benefit of practicing *ānāpānasati* is that we are able to practice in accordance with the principle of *paticca-samuppāda* (dependent co-origination, conditioned co-arising). The theory of
*paticca-samuppāda* is complex and lengthy. For those unfamiliar
with it, conditioned co-arising explains the causal origination of
*dukkha*. A series of causes, each dependent on a previous cause, leads
to suffering. Lord Buddha taught many variations on this theme,

but because of its great subtlety and profundity it is difficult to understand. Nonetheless, it is worth making an effort to study it.[11] Once we come to its practical application, however, dependent co-origination is exquisitely simple. In practice, it means having *sati* in the moment of *phassa* (sense contact). That is all. *Phassa* is the meeting of an internal sense organ, a corresponding external sense object, and the appropriate type of sense consciousness (*viññāna*). Simply having *sati* in the moment of *phassa* completely solves all the possible problems of *paticca-samuppāda*. In other words, before conditioned co-arising can develop, *sati* should be right there at the moment of contact. Do not let it be ignorant *phassa*. If *sati* is present, then that contact will not lead to ignorant feeling and ignorant feeling will not lead to foolish craving (*tanhā*). It will all stop right there at contact. This is another advantage of training in *ānāpānasati*: it makes *sati* sufficiently abundant, fast, and capable of performing its duty in the moment of *phassa* to stop the stream of *paticca-samuppāda* right then and there. This is an enormous benefit of practicing *ānāpānasati*.

Yet another benefit is that we are able to practice according to the principles of the four *ariya-sacca* with ease and completeness. We know about the Four Noble Truths. The essence of this set of laws is that *dukkha* is born out of ignorant desire (*tanhā*). If there is *tanhā*, there must be *dukkha*. When we use *sati* to stop *tanhā* and to cut it off, there is no *dukkha*. Through preventing ignorant sense experience (*phassa*), there is no ignorant feeling (*vedanā*) and *tanhā* is not stirred up. This is the most beneficial way to practice the Four Noble Truths. You can stop *tanhā* through the speed and power of the *sati* that you have developed by practicing *ānāpānasati* in all four tetrads.

## THE HEART OF THE TRIPLE GEM

A further benefit is that *ānāpānasati* easily, completely, and perfectly brings us the Triple Gem (*tiratana*), the Three Refuges of Buddhism. This is because the essence or nucleus of Buddha, Dhamma, and Sangha is in cleanliness, clarity, and calm. The state of *citta* that is clean, clear, and calm is the essence of Buddha, Dhamma, and Sangha. Please be careful about these three words. Lord Buddha is not some physical body or image. Rather, the state of mind that is clean, clear, and calm is the true Lord Buddha. In seeing the Dhamma, the Buddha is seen. The heart of the Dhamma is this cleanliness, clarity, and calmness itself. Then, the Sangha are those who through successful practice have clean, clear, and calm minds. All three words are very important. The first person to realize perfect cleanliness, clarity, and calm is called "Buddha," the truth that is realized is called "Dhamma," and those people who follow and practice accordingly are called "Sangha." When we practice *ānāpānasati*, we make our *citta* clean, clear, and calm, as we have explained in detail throughout this book. These qualities are the fruit of *virāga*, *nirodha*, and *patinissagga* (steps fourteen through sixteen). Through them there is cleanliness, clarity, and calmness; thus, we can say the genuine Buddha, Dhamma, and Sangha are in our hearts. This is another of the unsurpassed benefits of *ānāpānasati*.

## BUDDHISM IN ITS ENTIRETY

The next benefit in practicing *ānāpānasati* is that we practice the most fundamental principles of Buddhism, namely, *sīla*, *samādhi*, and *paññā*. These three factors are wholly present in the practitioner of *ānāpānasati*.

The unshakable determination to practice is *sīla* (virtue). Moreover, when the mind is set on correct action, that too is *sīla*. In the intention necessary to practice every step of *ānāpānasati* there is a natural *sīla*, automatically, without our having to specifically practice it. Then there is *samādhi* (concentration) as well. Because of this intention, we practice until *samādhi* arises. Then *paññā* (wisdom) develops, especially in the fourth tetrad, in which we contemplate the most perfect wisdom. In practicing *ānāpānasati* correctly the most fundamental principle of Buddhism is fulfilled; it leads to *sīla*, *samādhi*, and *paññā* in full measure. This is an enormous benefit: practicing Buddhism in its entirety.

When we study Buddhism in more detail, we learn about the seven *bojjhanga* (factors of awakening). In the *Ānāpānasati Sutta*, the Buddha asserts that fully practicing the sixteen steps of *ānāpānasati* perfects the four *satipaṭṭhāna* (applications of mindfulness). Through the perfection of the four *satipaṭṭhāna* (the subjects of the four tetrads—body, feeling, mind, and Dhamma), the seven *bojjhaṅga* are perfected. Then full awakening is assured. The seven *bojjhaṅga* are the very factors that lead to the enlightenment of the *arahant* (a human being who is liberated from all *dukkha*). It would take another book to go into all the details. For now we will simply list the names of these factors: *sati*, *dhammavicaya* (investigation of Dhamma), *viriya* (effort), *pīti* (contentment, satisfaction), *passaddhi* (tranquility), *samādhi* (concentration, collectedness), and *upekkhā* (equanimity, even-mindedness). When *ānāpānasati* is complete, these seven factors are complete. When these seven factors are complete, perfect awakening is assured. Although there is not enough space to explain further, we should understand that the seven *bojjhaṅga* are a certainty when we practice *ānāpānasati* completely. The recorded words of the Buddha clearly state this.[12] You can verify its truth by yourself.

### *NIBBĀNA* HERE AND NOW

The greatest possible benefit of the practice of mindfulness with breathing is that without having to die we will have *nibbāna* in this very life. By this is meant *nibbāna* here and now, having nothing to do with death. *Nibbāna* means "coolness." The word *nibbuto* also means "coolness," referring to a temporary coolness, not yet continual, not yet perfect. Nevertheless, the flavor is the same as perfect *nibbāna*. *Nibbuto* is like the sample a salesman shows of a product that we might actually buy. They must be alike. So we have a sample of *nibbāna* to taste for a little while. It is called temporary *nibbāna* or *sāmāyika-nibbāna*.

Coolness can also be the *nibbāna* that happens due to "that factor." In Pali it is called "that factor," which means something like "coincidental." For example, when there is *sati* focusing on the breath, the *citta* is cool. *Ānāpānasati* is "that factor," the agent, the cause, that brings about the coolness here and now. This is *tadadga-nibbāna*, coincidental *nibbāna*. This coolness occurs because there is no defilement; when there is no defilement, the *citta* is cool. When there is no fire, there is coolness. Here *ānāpānasati* eliminates the fires, that is, the defilements. Although it is only temporary, the fires disperse and there is coolness for a while. There is *nibbāna* for a period due to "that factor," that tool, namely *ānāpānasati*. Although momentary, not yet perfect and perpetual, the flavor of *nibbāna* is savored as a sample, a taste. *Ānāpānasati* helps us to sample *nibbāna* little by little, moment by moment, during this very life. And nothing has to die! Then, the duration of that coolness is lengthened, its extent broadened, and its frequency increased until there is perfect *nibbāna*. If attained, this benefit is the most satisfying, the most worthwhile.

It is important that we correctly understand this word *nibbāna*. It means "cool" and has nothing to do with dying. We use the term *parinibbāna* if we are referring to the kind of *nibbāna* associated with death, such as the death of an *arahant*. Just *nibbāna* without the prefix "*pari*" simply means "cool," the absence of heat. Imagine that everything is going right for you: you have good health, economic security, a good family, good friends, and good surroundings. Then, according to the meaning of *nibbāna*, this life of yours is cool. It may not be perfect *nibbāna*, because to be perfect it must include a cool mind, but it is cool just the same.

*Nibbāna* means "cool." We can even use this word with regard to material things. A burning charcoal that gradually cools down until it is no longer hot is said to *nibbāna*. When soup is too hot to eat, we wait for it to cool off; we then say that the soup is *nibbāna* enough to consume. We might even apply it to fierce and dangerous animals captured from the forest, then tamed and trained until fully domesticated. They too can be said to *nibbāna*. In the Pali texts, *nibbāna* is used regarding material things, animals, and people. If something is cool rather than hot, it is *nibbāna* in one sense or another. And it need not die. Through practicing *ānāpānasati* we will receive the most satisfying sort of *nibbāna*—cool in body, cool in mind, cool in all aspects.

In short, we have a cool life here and now; our life is *nibbāna* in the sense just discussed. In Pali, this is called *nibbuto*, meaning "one who is cooled" or "one who has *nibbāna*." This reality is called *nibbāna*. This kind of person is called *nibbuto*.

## THE LAST BREATH

There are many other benefits of practicing *ānāpānasati* that we could cite, but space does not permit it. One last item, however, should be mentioned: we will know the last breath of our life. That is, we will know the breath in which we will die. This does not mean that we will choose the moment of our death; it just means that by becoming well versed in our practice of *ānāpānasati* we will become experts regarding the breath. We will know instantly whether we are going to die during this present breath or not. Thus, we will be able to predict the final breath of our life.

Lord Buddha himself declared that he realized Perfect Self-Awakening (*anuttara sammāsambodhi*) through the practice of *ānāpānasati*. So he offered it to us as the best system to practice. He advised us to use this practice for our own welfare, for the welfare of others, for the welfare of everyone. There is no better way to practice Dhamma than mindfulness with breathing. May you give careful attention to it.

Our discussion of *ānāpānasati-bhāvana* is now sufficiently complete. We conclude this final chapter here, and with it the teaching on mindfulness with breathing for serious beginners.

# Translator's Conclusion:
# Summary and Suggestions for Practice

Following Ajahn Buddhadāsa's lectures, the translator was asked to give a summary. Based on the experience of the ongoing retreat, emphasis was placed on attitudes and techniques that would help beginners get off to a correct start. The following section is based on that talk.

I WILL ATTEMPT TO REVIEW and add to some of the main points from the preceding chapters, mainly those with which our Western readers might have the most trouble and confusion. Some of these are practical hints and tips to use in establishing the practice of *ānāpānasati*. The rest involve right view (*sammā-diṭṭhi*). The more our attitude is correct, the more our practice of *ānāpānasati* will be correct and will lead to the quenching of all *dukkha* through the end of attachment. Although I do not claim to be a meditation master, I hope that this information will be of some practical benefit to you. It is based on the experience of leading *ānāpānasati* monthly for many years, frequent discussions with Ajahn Buddhadāsa, and personal practice.

## NATURAL EVOLUTION/INTENTIONAL PRACTICE

Let's begin with a distinction that is generally overlooked. When we talk about *ānāpānasati*, we also talk about a natural evolution of the mind, of human life. This natural evolution is not the same as our meditation practice, although the two happen together and mutually support each other. The sixteen steps of *ānāpānasati* are based on the contemplation of sixteen distinct objects (including, but not limited to, the breath) while we maintain awareness of breathing in and breathing out. In our study of life, we focus on these sixteen living objects. At the same time, these sixteen objects arise naturally out of our cultivation of the mind (*citta-bhāvanā*). The mind must follow a certain path of evolution from wherever it "is" to what is called "awakening" or "liberation." This path is fundamentally the same for all beings, a natural evolution that is both the duty and the privilege of us all. *Ānāpānasati* meditation is not that evolution itself; rather, *ānāpānasati* is the studying and nurturing of that evolution. As that evolution takes place—and it has already begun—we use *ānāpānasati* to study and understand it. Through that understanding we can use *ānāpānasati* to further support, nurture, and nudge that evolution along. Thus, the practice and the progress are interconnected and inseparable but not identical.

People often confuse the two. We often hear, "Oh! I had rapture, I got *pīti*, I had contentment. I must be on step five." The same confusion occurs regarding most of the steps, and some of us think that we are doing them all in one short sitting. The feeling of contentment, as well as the other objects, will be arising all the time, coming and going all the time, part of the natural process that is taking place. In step five, however, we only start to work with *pīti* at the proper time, which is after the first four steps have been completed and *pīti* manifests clearly and steadily. Even while we are practicing step one, feelings of contentment and joy arise to some degree. This is nothing to get excited about. We might even become aware of impermanence during step one, but that is not step thirteen unless we intentionally contemplate that impermanence. (In the case of impermanence, if it is a genuine insight and not just talking to oneself, it is worth following up immediately. With the first twelve steps, however, it is best to take them patiently, one at a time.) At any one time, we have the intention to practice one specific step or object. All other objects are to be left alone. If the mind should wander, merely note it, let go, and return to the current object or lesson while breathing in and out.

There is this difference between what is happening naturally and what we are practicing specifically. To summarize, on the natural side there are the sixteen objects that occur naturally whenever the conditions are present. On the practical side, we systematically contemplate and train upon these sixteen things one by one. Please be clear about this. It will help you to know what you need to do and when, and to practice efficiently.

Another aspect of this natural evolution is that the mind evolves from cruder states of happiness to more subtle states of happiness.

When we begin meditating, we are still interested in rather crude kinds of happiness, usually sensual and sexual happiness. Through meditation we come across refined levels of joy. As *citta-bhāvanā* continues, we discover even more sublime levels of bliss. Once we learn of a higher or more refined level of happiness, then it is quite easy to let go of the coarser kinds. Thus, in this practice there is a natural progression of the mind letting go of a crude happiness through the discovery of a better happiness. Then the mind becomes attached to that better happiness until it finds an even higher level of joy. It can then let go of what is now a lower level of happiness to enjoy the higher level. This proceeds by fits and starts until we learn that supreme happiness is not to become attached to or indulge in any form of happiness.

## One Step at a Time, Please

*Ānāpānasati* must be practiced one step at a time. We only get confused and distracted by trying to do two or more things at once. We should be satisfied with the step we are on and be willing to practice correctly, for as long as it takes. We should not jump around from this step to that, merely because we are restless, bored, or full of desires. Do not listen when you find yourself thinking, "Today I'll try all sixteen steps," or "Let's do the first tetrad this week, and the second next week, and then the third," or "What if I start with sixteen and work backwards?" Don't just leaf through this book and choose something that interests you. We must take the lessons one by one, because *ānāpānasati* is based on the natural evolution already described. To make the most of this natural fact, it is best to follow *ānāpānasati* as it has been taught by the Buddha.

We should always start at the beginning. Each session starts with firmly establishing *sati* in the breathing and then practicing step one. After you are skilled in step one, after you know it well and can do it with ease, then go on to step two. Practice step two until you are expert in it and have learned what you need to know about it. Then, you can go to step three. Do not fall into the confusion of a little of step one, then a bit of step two, then some of this and some of that. We are often impatient with where we are and want to get somewhere else. We would be wise to restrain that urge.

Practice the steps one at a time, remaining with each step until you are an expert in it.

Each session is brand new. Each sitting or walking period is brand new. In fact, each breath is new. So each session must start with step one. Even if you were working with step three or four yesterday, or before lunch, unless you have kept it going throughout the interim, you must start at the beginning, as is only natural. If you have already succeeded with step one, now you must review it at the start of each session until the knowledge of it is directly here and now, rather than mere memory. Each step must be reviewed in the same way to make sure that we are expert in it right now. Depending on conditions—primarily internal—some sessions will not get past step one and others will get as far as our overall progress. We never know until we do it. Without expectation we practice step by step, seeing what happens and learning what we can.

This is merely the way things are. Each step depends on the previous steps. The conditions for step five are the completion of steps one through four. We are ready for step ten only when we have gone through the first nine successfully. Once we can accept things as they are, we can stop desiring that they be otherwise. By accepting the nature of these steps—that is, the nature of our own bodies, breathing, and minds—we can practice wisely, without impatience, boredom, and frustration.

### PATIENCE AND PROGRESS

Finally, let's remember that *khanti* (patience, endurance) is a necessary spiritual tool. The Buddha said:

> Patient endurance is the supreme incinerator of
> defilement.
> *(Khantī paramaṁ tapo titikkhā)* [13]

We are often in the habit of judging and measuring ourselves against various standards. Some of us are competitive and judge ourselves according to others. Sometimes we judge ourselves according to the various ideals we have. Many people, when they learn about the sixteen steps of *ānāpānasati*, judge themselves according to these steps. We foolishly think, "I am a better person when practicing step four than when practicing only step one." We all want to be good and practice step four and then five and then six. Such thinking will not do us any good.

Do not measure progress according to these sixteen steps. Measure progress according to the development of spiritual qualities, such as *sati*, perseverance, understanding, confidence, calmness, friendliness, compassion, balance, and so forth. Measure it against the diminishing of attachment and the disappearance of greed, anger, and delusion. These results of correct practice will increase noticeably even during step one. Even if we stick with little old step one for the rest of our lives, if we do it properly, these qualities will grow and attachment will diminish. There will be less and less *dukkha*, and that is all that matters.

Getting to step sixteen is not so important. In fact, step one can be enough. The reality of *nibbāna* is unconditioned and not caught within time. So you never know when *nibbāna* will be realized; maybe even during step one. You need not hurry to get on to steps two or three or ten. Step one might be enough if you just do it right. Do it with patience, with balance, with clarity, with wisdom. Do it without clinging and grasping. Just do it.

We find that when we have more patience and endurance in our *ānāpānasati* practice, then patience and endurance are more a part of our daily lives. They help us to live a clean, clear, calm life. So let us be very, very patient. Learn to sit still. Learn to forget about all those "things that I have to do." Learn to keep plugging away at step one until it is complete. And then proceed to step two. Do each step properly and do not hurry. With patience the mind will develop, it will "get somewhere." As long as there is impatience and desire to move on, you are learning little of consequence and experiencing much *dukkha*.

Regarding attitude or right view: discover the natural evolution; study it systematically; always start anew; take things one step at a time; be patient; put aside expectations, desires, and demands; stay balanced; learn to identify and let go of the attachments that creep into your practice. In short, practice to understand *dukkha* and to realize the end of *dukkha*. Accept that *nibbāna* is the reason for practicing *ānāpānasati* and be delighted with this great opportunity.

## Getting Started: Establishing *Sati*

Any practice of *citta-bhāvanā* begins with taking up *sati* and establishing it upon the initial meditation object; thus, we begin by establishing *sati* on our first object, the breath. This can be called the "preliminary step," or "lesson zero," if we wish to number it. There are various ways of being mindful of the breath. We can arrange them progressively from coarse to subtle in a way that corresponds to the first four steps. The following is a simple approach that should work well for most people, but you need not follow it blindly. As always, you must find what works best for you. Remember, never go by mere opinions or biases, learn from experience.

(1) Once you are seated comfortably and are relaxed and still, feel the breathing, which is now easily noted within the quiet and still body. Direct attention to the breathing in a firm and gentle way. Maintain this watchfulness of the breathing and become familiar with both the breathing and the mindfulness of it. This attention to the breathing can be general, that is, not focused on any one specific place.

(2) Note the three primary segments of each breath: beginning, middle, and end. During the inhalation these correspond to the nose, the middle of the chest, and the abdomen. During the exhalation the reverse is true, beginning at the belly and ending at the nose. Watch and wait at the nose until the incoming breath is felt there. Then, skip to the middle of the chest and watch there until the breath is felt. Next, skip to the abdomen and watch there until the breath is felt. Continue watching as the inhalation ends and wait for the exhalation to begin. Once the exhalation is felt at the abdomen, go to the middle of the chest and then to the nose. Observe at the nose as the exhalation ends and wait for the new inhalation to be felt, then skip to the chest, and so on. With *sati*, note the breath at each of these points as it passes in and out, in and out. Be careful to patiently observe at each point until the breathing (the movement of the breath itself or of the organs used for breathing) is felt. Only then does the mind jump to the next point. This hopping from point to point is a relatively easy way to establish *sati* on the breath. It is a good way to get started. It becomes, however, somewhat crude and agitating after a while. Once we are skilled at

it, we will want a more refined and peaceful way to be mindful of the breath.

(3) Next, we connect the three points into a continuous sweep or flow. This more closely approximates the breath itself. We call this "following, chasing, hunting, stalking." While breathing naturally, without any forcing or manipulating of the breath, *sati* follows the breath in and out, between the tip of the nose and the navel. Follow the breath, do not lead it. Track the succession of physical sensations—which must be felt, experienced—in and out.

(4) Once following becomes easy and constant, it will begin to feel unnecessarily busy and disruptive. Now we are ready for guarding, a more peaceful way to practice *sati* with the breathing. By this time, a certain point in the nose will stand out. This is right where the breath is felt most clearly and distinctly. Although some people may feel that there are two points, one in each nostril, do not make things unnecessarily complicated. Simply note one point that covers both nostrils. This is called the "guarding point." We choose a point in the nose because it is more subtle, exact, and distinct than other places such as the abdomen or chest where the movements are large and coarse. To calm the breath, we must use a point that is small, focused, and suitably refined. With *sati*, fix the *citta* on this point. Allow the *citta* to gather itself at this point. Do so by simultaneously calming the breath and becoming more sensitive (through *sati*) to the increasingly subtle sensations at the guarding point. Continue to calm the body-conditioner until proper and sufficient *samādhi* develops.

We can always begin with the first technique. The second and third techniques are suitable for steps one and two. Step three is best done by following, although guarding can also be used. Step four should begin with following and then take up guarding.

If at first our breaths are short and shallow, with movement in the chest only and not in the abdomen, then simply follow the breath down as far as it goes. After *sati* is established, we will relax and the breathing will become deeper. Just sitting still for ten or fifteen minutes also helps. Before long we will feel movement in the abdomen. If we see that the breath is passing by many places at the same time, do not use this as an opportunity to complicate matters.

Keep it simple. A simple flow from the tip of the nose to the navel and from the navel to the tip of the nose is sufficient for our purposes. Do not look for or create complex breathing patterns. Do not try to watch every separate movement at once. If we merely observe the breath, the process will remain simple. If we spend our time thinking about the breath, it is easy to get confused.

This is a good opportunity to emphasize that *sati* is not "thinking about" something. *Sati* is reflective attention, awareness, watchfulness, observance, scrutiny. There is no need for concepts, labels, words, and pictures. Such things only get in the way of directly experiencing the breathing in and out. We can compare "following" the breath to walking along a river. The water flows; we walk along and watch it flow. We need not talk to ourselves, "river, river—flowing, flowing—this, that—blah, blah, blah," to see the river. In such a case, if we are not careful, we will stop watching the river and get lost in our words and thoughts. We do enough of that already. Why bring it into our *ānāpānasati* practice, too?

## TRICKS TO AID *SATI*

If it is too much of a struggle to keep the mind on the breath while following, there are some tricks or aids we can use. The first is to aim the eyes at the tip of the nose, as Ajahn Buddhadāsa suggests. Do this in a relaxed and gentle way. Do not cross the eyes or create tensions; this will only lead to headaches, not to *sati*. At first you may be able only to gaze a little beyond or in front of the nose, but as the body and face relax, you will be able to gaze at the tip itself. Even when the eyelids are closed, we can aim the eyes at the tip of the nose.

A second trick is to breathe loudly. Breathe loud and strong enough to hear the breath. The ears as well as the eyes can support *sati*. This can be particularly useful at the beginning of a session or after a disturbance. After following is established, we naturally drop the loud breathing as it will become annoying. You should try some loud breathing, however, at the beginning of a session or whenever you find it difficult to establish *sati*.

The third trick is counting. We can gang up on the breath with the eyes, the ears, and now the intellect. Count each inhalation as it begins, one number for each breath. If the mind wanders, start over with "one." If we can count to "ten" without the mind wandering, go back to "one" anyway. For our purposes here, a simple count of each breath is enough. The method of counting explained by Ajahn Buddhadāsa serves another purpose and comes later. Again, once *sati* is well established, counting is unnecessary and should be dropped. With training, *sati* becomes more subtle, alert, and natural.

These tricks are to help us get started and should not be confused with lessons one, two, and so on. After becoming familiar with them, you will always have them at your service, whether in meditation or ordinary life.

### LONG AND SHORT BREATHS

As *sati* is established (techniques two or three), we begin to notice the long and short breathing. The mind may occasionally still wander, but it stays with the breath enough to learn what the breath is like. The first and easiest quality to note is length, in terms of both time and extent of physical movement. For our purposes, an exact dividing line between short and long is not important. Become familiar with your own breathing and learn what your longest breaths and shortest breaths are like relative to each other. There is no need to compare your breath to anyone else's.

Generally, you will find that abdominal breathing is longer than chest breathing, that is, if abdominal breathing comes naturally. This is something we observe, however; it is not something we desire or force. We are not "supposed" to breathe in a certain way, and we do not use *ānāpānasati* to develop any special way of breathing. So do not try to force abdominal breathing since the results would not be very relaxing. When abdominal breathing occurs naturally, however, you will see that it is longer, more relaxed, and healthier.

In fact, long breathing is more "not doing" than "doing." In other words, don't hurry the inhalation or squeeze out the exhalation. Let the inhalation naturally flow in by itself; the body knows exactly how to do it. Release the exhalation naturally, without pushing it out or cutting it off abruptly. Both require a relaxed diaphragm and abdomen, so let go of all those tensions down there.

It is important to be patient during the transitions from inhalation to exhalation and from exhalation to inhalation. Watch carefully but gently as one ends, and wait calmly for the next to begin by itself.

Should your breaths become very long, you will discover an interesting point. You may have thought it strange when Ajahn Buddhadāsa said that the chest expands and the abdomen contracts with the long in-breath. Common sense says that the abdomen expands on the in-breath and contracts on the out-breath; common sense seems to contradict Ajahn Buddhadāsa. Which is right? First, we observe normal breathing: as we inhale, the diaphragm drops and pushes the tummy outward; when we exhale, the tummy falls in again. This is ordinary abdominal breathing before it becomes very long. It is a simple movement of the abdomen expanding (or rising) with the in-breath and contracting (or falling) with the out-breath. Some people will consider this short whereas others will feel it is relatively long.

Now, there is a limit to how far the abdomen can expand. As we relax and breath more deeply, this limit will be reached. At that point there is, however, room left in the lungs for more air. If we continue to breathe in, the chest will then expand. This, in turn, pulls up and flattens the tummy. This is what Ajahn Buddhadāsa referred to. A very long inhalation begins just like a normal breath; the abdomen expands but the chest barely moves at all. After the abdomen's limit is reached the chest expands and the abdomen contracts. When the breath is really long, you will discover this for yourself. The opposite movements occur (roughly) with the very long exhalations. So, the very long breath is an ordinary breath plus more. Until the body becomes very relaxed through *ānāpānasati*, many of us will seldom experience this very long breathing. Eventually, it will happen more and more regularly—even outside formal sittings.

Any breathing that is less than long can be considered short. There are a few ways, however, to describe short breathing in more detail. The first is that if it feels short to you, then it *is* short. Such a definition may be helpful for neophytes. The second definition is more precise; chest breathing, breathing in which all the movement is in the chest with little or none in the abdomen, is clearly short and shallow (and usually rather fast). The third description is most appropriate for those who are committed to a long-term practice of *ānāpānasati*. The "normal breath" discussed above is considered short; that is, anything less than a full long breath that expands the belly and then the chest is short. When starting out, be flexible about the distinction between long and short. As you gain experience, you'll find the third definition to be the most useful.

Even when *sati* is less than firmly established, we will be learning about long and short breathing. Steps one and two really begin, however, when *sati* can follow the breath without faltering. Sounds, thoughts, and other phenomena may occasionally wander through, but the mind does not get caught up in them. We are able to stay with the breath, observe it, and learn. If the mind still wanders a great deal, consider yourself to be on the "preliminary step," that is, still getting started. Focus attention solely on establishing *sati* on the in-breaths and out-breaths. Until you are successful, that should be your only concern.

If we are impatient to get through step one and want to move on to "more interesting things," we can check such thoughts by asking ourselves: "Is the body relaxed enough to sit like this for an hour or more, comfortably, without any desire to move?" When the breathing is truly long, it is possible to sit comfortably for long periods of time. If we are restlessly changing positions every ten or fifteen minutes, it is best to be content with step one. Learn how to sit still, relax, and allow the breath to become long, slow, gentle, and smooth. Then, we will be able to sit for long periods of time with ease. This requires self-discipline—not self-torture. Train yourself wisely, with balance.

## STEP THREE: A NEW OBJECT

In steps one and two the breathing is the only object of our attention. Beginning with step three, we take up other objects, in this case "all bodies." Here, we focus on the influence of the breathing upon the rest of the body. Note that the focus is no longer the breathing itself, although the breathing and its influence are closely associated. At this time, the awareness of breathing in and out moves into the background where it remains clear and constant.

While the mind focuses on the new object, we always know whether we are breathing in or out. This holds true for the rest of the sixteen steps.

Studying the influence of the breathing upon the body involves more than just long and short breaths. Length was a convenient way to begin. Now, we should also notice speed (fast-slow) and texture (coarse-subtle). Texture, or quality, is the most important because it has the greatest influence on the calmness of the body. In this step, we will discover the kind of breathing that most effectively calms the body. Then we are ready for step four.

### LIFE IS MEDITATION

These suggestions and tips should be enough to help you get started and to develop a wise meditation practice. Please note the following observations as well.

There is more to meditation (*citta-bhāvanā*, mental cultivation) than sitting. Our formal sitting and walking practice is very important, and there are few people who do not need it, but we are interested, most of all, in living life—life free of *dukkha*. Our lives involve more than sitting, and *ānāpānasati* can help us in other areas of life as well.

First, the skills and knowledge developed through formal practice can be used and expanded upon throughout our daily activities. Second, we can be aware of, if not concentrated on, the breath while performing most duties. If this is developed properly, the breath regulates the body in a state of correctness and anchors the mind in purity, stability, tranquility, clarity, strength, and alertness. Third, the mind can go to the breath and focus upon it when harmful mental states arise. In doing so, the breath should not be treated as an escape. Nevertheless, it is often the most skillful means out of an unwholesome thought, emotion, or mood.

As you grow to love this practice and its benefits, you will seek out opportunities to practice whenever you can. This can be frustrating, however, in our busy, time-poor world. Fortunately, a wonderful quality of *ānāpānasati* is that we can practice it anywhere without doing anything special. For example, when finding yourself waiting in a line or office, or at a traffic light, don't waste your precious time being bored or nervous! Practice *ānāpānasati*, at least until the light turns green. There is no need to close your eyes or to sit in a way that draws attention to yourself. You can practice while standing or in whatever position you may find yourself. When making a telephone call to somebody, there is time for a few mindful breaths even while waiting for that person to pick up the phone. Computers often make us wait: a chance to come back to the reality of breathing in and out, of being alive and awake. You can probably find a couple hours for such practice even in your busiest day. These are just a few ways to integrate *ānāpānasati* into your life as a whole.

## SATIPAṬṬHĀNA IS ĀNĀPĀNASATI

Even the theory of *ānāpānasati* can be used throughout the meditation of daily life. Once we have taken the time to study and understand the sixteen steps (which may involve some supplementary reading), we need not limit their application to breathing alone. Ajahn Buddhadāsa points out that both versions of the *Satipaṭṭhāna Sutta*[14] lack a clearly defined method of practice, whereas the *Ānāpānasati Sutta* outlines a complete progressive system of practice:

> Another common problem is that some people cling to and are stuck on the word *satipaṭṭhāna* (foundations of mindfulness) far too much. Some go so far as to think that *ānāpānasati* has nothing to do with the four foundations of mindfulness. Some even reject *ānāpānasati* out of hand. In some places they really hang onto the word *satipaṭṭhāna*. They cling to the *satipaṭṭhāna* of the *Dīgha-nikāya* (*Long Discourses*), which is nothing more than a long list of names, a lengthy catalog of sets of dhammas. Although there are whole groups of dhammas, no method of practice is given or explained. This is what is generally taken to be *satipaṭṭhāna*. Then it is adjusted and rearranged into different practices, which become new systems that are called *satipaṭṭhāna* practices or meditation.[15]
>
> Then, the followers of such techniques deny, or even despise, the *ānāpānasati* approach, asserting that it is not *satipaṭṭhāna*. In truth, *ānāpānasati* is the heart of *satipaṭṭhāna*, the heart of all four foundations of mindfulness. The sixteen

steps are a straightforward and clear practice, not just a list of names or dhammas, like in the *Mahāsatipaṭṭhāna Sutta* (*Digha-nikāya* 22). Therefore, let us not fall into the misunderstanding that *ānāpānasati* is not *satipaṭṭhāna*; otherwise, we might lose interest in it, thinking that it is wrong. Unfortunately, this misunderstanding is common. Let us reiterate that *ānāpānasati* is the heart of all four *satipaṭṭhāna* in a form that can be readily practiced.

We have taken time to consider the words *satipaṭṭhāna* and *ānāpānasati* for the sake of ending any misunderstandings that might lead to a narrow-minded lack of consideration for what others are practicing. So please understand correctly that whether we call it *satipaṭṭhāna* or *ānāpānasati* there are only four matters of importance: *kāya, vedanā, citta*, and Dhamma. However, in the *Mahāsatipaṭṭhāna Sutta* there's no explanation of how to practice these four things. It only gives and expands upon the names of *dhammas*. For example, the matter of *kāya* (body) is spread out over corpse meditations, *satisampajaññā* in daily activities, the postures, and other things, more than can be remembered. This sutta merely catalogs groups of *dhammas* under the four areas of study.

The *Ānāpānasati Sutta*, on the other hand, shows how to practice the four foundations in a systematic progression that ends with emancipation from all *dukkha*. The sixteen steps work through the four foundations, each one developing upon the previous one and supporting the next. If you practice all sixteen steps fully, the heart of the *satipaṭṭhāna* arises perfectly. In short, the *satipaṭṭhāna* suttas are simply lists of names. The *Ānāpānasati Sutta* clearly shows how to practice the four foundations without anything extra or surplus, without mentioning unrelated matters.[16]

The four foundations and mindfulness of them are the basis for all meditation practice; we should at every opportunity work to develop the four foundations of mindfulness. You will see that the sixteen steps provide a general structure for all *satipaṭṭhāna* practice. These are the sixteen things that we should contemplate every chance we can, whenever these *dhammas* occur. Although most bodily processes are not open to the systematic and complete treatment we use with the breathing, we can use the sixteen steps to identify the things most worthy of our attention.

### CONDENSED VERSION

Some people may feel intimidated or put off by all the steps. In this regard, Ajahn Buddhadāsa has given the following advice:

> If some people feel that sixteen steps are too much, that is all right. It is possible to condense the sixteen down to two steps. One—train the *citta* (mind) to be adequately and properly concentrated. Two—with that *samādhi*, skip over to contemplate *aniccaṁ, dukkhaṁ*, and *anattā* right away. Just these two steps, if they are performed with every inhalation and exhalation, can also be considered *ānāpānasati*. If you do not like the complete sixteen-steps practice, or if you think that it is too theoretical, too much to study, or too detailed, then just take these two steps. Concentrate the *citta* by contemplating the breath. When you feel that there is sufficient *samādhi*, examine everything that you know and experience so that you realize how they are impermanent, how they are unsatisfactory, and how they are not-self. Just this much is enough to get the desired results, namely—letting go! release! no attachment! Finally, note the ending of *kilesa* (defilement) and the ceasing of attachment when you fully see *aniccaṁ-dukkhaṁ*. Thus, you can take this short approach if you wish.
>
> Here, however, we want you to understand the complete system; thus, we must speak about the sixteen-step practice. Once you fully understand the entire sixteen steps, you can abridge them for yourself. Decrease them until you are satisfied enough to practice with confidence. You might end up with two steps, or five steps, or whatever suits you. This is our purpose in the way we explain *ānāpānasati*. We explain the system of practice in full, then you can shorten it for yourself depending on what pleases you.
>
> This is why we have studied and explained the sixteen-step method in full, because it will reveal the secrets of nature through its scientific approach. This is a science that leads to a

natural understanding of *kāya, vedanā, citta,* and Dhamma, in the best and most complete way possible, through the perspective and approach of natural science. This method is a scientific approach that can regulate these four things. First, study the complete sixteen steps, then you may trim them down by yourself. Choose for yourself what you need. Practice only two or three steps if you want. Keep just two or three or five steps as you like.[17]

## THE SHORTCUT METHOD FOR ORDINARY PEOPLE

We will begin by speaking for those who do not like "a lot." By "a lot" they seem to mean too much, or a surplus. Well, the surplus is not necessary. We will take just what is sufficient for ordinary people, which is called "the shortcut method." The essence of this method is to adequately concentrate the mind, which any ordinary person can do, and then take that concentrated citta to observe *aniccaṁ-dukkhaṁ-anattā*—the three characteristics of being—until realizing *suññatā* and *tathatā*. With this practice it is possible to realize the benefits of *samādhi* as well as the full-scale result of extinguishing *dukkha,* but there will not be any additional special qualities. Such special abilities are not necessary anyway. Therefore, make the mind sufficiently concentrated, then examine *aniccaṁ* and *dukkhaṁ*. Just practice sufficiently the first tetrad of *ānāpānasati,* then practice sufficiently the fourth tetrad. That is all! Sufficient is not a lot, nor is it good enough. This is the shortcut for ordinary people.

Now let's look at the method of practicing the first tetrad. If you make the breath fine, the entire body will be subtle, that is, tranquil and cool. Just this much is sufficient for having a mind good enough to do *vipassanā*. Then the *citta* is on a level that it can use to contemplate *aniccaṁ-dukkhaṁ-anattā,* which manifests in every part and particle of our bodies. We contemplate the impermanence, unsatisfactoriness, and selflessness of every organ and component in our bodies—both concrete and mental—until we realize suchness. When we see suchness, we do not fall under the power of dualism. It is enough. This much is enough to penetrate higher and higher into the Dhamma until realizing the highest. This is the shortcut for ordinary people. Those living in the common, ordinary world—even those living the household life—are able to do at least this much.[18]

## SIXTEEN STEPS TO EVERYTHING

We can use any bodily activity as a basis for *sati*. The more necessary and central to life (like breathing) that activity is, the better. First, get to know that activity from all angles (long-short may or may not be relevant). Second, see what influence that activity has on the flesh-body. Third, find the right way to perform that activity so that it has the optimal effect on the body and allows the mind to find an appropriate degree and type of concentration. This corresponds to the first tetrad (*kāya*). Next, examine the feelings associated with that activity, especially the pleasant feelings that arise when the activity is done well and successfully. Study the influence these feelings have on the mind, then calm that influence. This covers the second tetrad (*vedanā*). The third tetrad (*citta*) begins with experiencing the different types of mind that arise during that activity. Then we train to gladden, concentrate, and liberate the mind while that activity is taking place. Finally, the fourth and most important tetrad (Dhamma) is to contemplate all aspects of that activity—body, feeling, and mind—as *aniccaṁ*, *dukkhaṁ*, and *anattā*. Contemplate the fading away and extinction of attachment. Contemplate the tossing back to nature of everything associated with that basic activity.

*Ānāpānasati* explains how to use everything we do as *satipaṭṭhāna* practice. When possible, practice *ānāpānasati* directly. Otherwise, practice it indirectly through a parallel practice. The knowledge we gain through parallel *citta-bhāvanā* will supplement and support our regular *ānāpānasati* practice, and vice versa. Once we appreciate the possibilities inherent in the sixteen steps, there will be constant opportunities to develop the *citta* even in the "most difficult conditions." The sixteen steps—especially the first and last tetrads—are enough meditation theory to eliminate *dukkha* from life. May you use them well.

## NOTHING SURPLUS

While simplified versions of *ānāpānasati* are common, Ajahn Buddha-dāsa maintains that the sixteen-step approach of the Buddha is the most effective.

> You can see for yourself whether it is a lot or not, surplus or not. We begin our study with *dukkha* itself and the cause of *dukkha's* arising. Then we study the foundations on which *dukkha* grows: the body and the *vedanā*. We go on to study that thing that experiences either *dukkha* or the absence of *dukkha*, namely, the *citta*. Lastly, we study Dhamma—the truth of all things—so that the *citta* knows, knows, knows, until it does not become attached to anything. Know letting go. There is a great deal to be done. To do it, our practice must be complete. Thus, we have the sixteen steps. As I explain it to you, it does not seem the least bit excessive. Really, there are so many matters to study and know in life that to have only sixteen steps is not very much at all. Some may say that it is too much, that they do not want to study and practice. If they do not think that it can help them, well, whatever suits them. Anyone who does not want to study and train in the complete sixteen steps can follow a condensed practice as previously explained. That is still enough to get something beneficial out of Buddhism through the technique of *samādhi-bhāvanā*.[19]

## LORD BUDDHA'S *VIPASSANĀ*

What is real *vipassanā*? Propaganda put out by certain meditation teachers might lead one to believe that only the meditation system of the speaker, or his teacher, can be considered to be *vipassanā*. Such insinuation is pure nonsense and leads to narrow-mindedness and confusion. There are, in fact, numerous approaches to *vipassanā*, and *ānāpānasati* is one of the most important. In fact, of the many approaches, *ānāpānasati* surely has the best claim to being Lord Buddha's approach. No other system is detailed in the suttas, whereas *ānāpānasati* has its own sutta, is partially discussed in the two *satipaṭṭhāna* suttas, and is prominent in the *Vinaya-piṭaka* and the *Saṁyutta-nikāya* as well. Such claims, however, are not the point. The sole point is whether a particular approach, when practiced correctly, brings a final end to *dukkha*. Such proof will be found in practice and realization rather than in sectarian arguments.

## SANGHA

A growing number of people are practicing *ānāpānasati* in some form, as well as other kinds of meditation, but do not always have regular access to qualified teachers. Everyone shares in the same joys and difficulties that you meet with in your practice. To join with some of the many meditators—they are everywhere, even in your area—to form a sitting group will be of great benefit to you, not to mention to the wider community. Sitting groups need not be large. It isn't necessary that you be "Buddhists" or that everyone practice in the same way, as long as you all sit quietly. The important things are mutual friendship, respect, and support, and that the group meet regularly, say, once a week. Such groups can help keep you going when times are rough or your spirit is weak. Further, they are a source of the community or sangha that we all need, especially in our hyper-individualistic, alienated modern societies. Imagine what the world would be like with meditation groups everywhere cultivating peace, compassion, and wisdom!

I hope that you are able to use this information. I have presented it as clearly as I am able. Please study it carefully; you may find that more than a few readings are necessary. Think it through sufficiently. Then, most importantly, try it. By practicing, your understanding of these instructions will grow. You will need to make adjustments, but for the most part those adjustments will be in your own understanding and application rather than in Ajahn Buddhadāsa's instructions. Try to follow his advice as well as you are able. Avoid mixing it with things you hear from meditators using other systems. With patience, dedication, and wisdom allow this practice to deepen and lead to the understanding of non-attachment and the realization of the end of *dukkha*, the supreme peace and freedom of *nibbāna*.

# Mindfulness with Breathing Discourse

(*Ānāpānasati Sutta*)[20]

## INTRODUCTION

I have heard thus:

At one time the Exalted One[21] was staying near Sāvatthī,[22] in the mansion of Migāra's mother in the Eastern Grove, together with many widely known elder disciples: Venerable Sāriputta, Venerable Mahā-Moggallāna, Venerable Mahā-Kassapa, Venerable Mahā-Kaccāyana, Venerable Mahā-Koṭṭhita, Venerable Mahā-Kappina, Venerable Mahā-Cunda, Venerable Revata, Venerable Ānanda, and other widely known elder disciples.

At that time those venerable elders taught and trained the new bhikkhus. Some of the elders taught and trained ten bhikkhus, some of them taught and trained thirty bhikkhus, and some of them taught and trained forty bhikkhus. Those new bhikkhus, when taught and trained by the elders so, understood that which is lofty and excellent more than ever before.

During that time the Exalted One was sitting in the open surrounded by the community of bhikkhus on the observance day of the fifteenth, the full moon night, of the last month of the rains residence.[23] The Exalted One surveyed the calm and silent assembly of bhikkhus, then spoke:

"Bhikkhus, we are certain of this way of practice. Bhikkhus, we are convinced by this way of practice. Bhikkhus, for this reason you should summon up even more energy for attaining the unattained, for reaching the unreached, for realizing the unrealized. I will wait here at Sāvatthī until the fourth and final month of the rains, the blossoming time of the white lotus (*komudī*)."

The bhikkhus in the countryside came to know that the Exalted One would remain at Sāvatthī until the fourth and final month of the rains, the blossoming time of the white lotus. They streamed continuously into Sāvatthī in order to attend upon the

Exalted One. Further, the venerable elders taught and trained the newly arrived bhikkhus in great measure. Some of the elders taught and trained ten bhikkhus, some of them taught and trained twenty bhikkhus, some of them taught and trained thirty bhikkhus, and some of them taught and trained forty bhikkhus. Those new bhikkhus, when taught and trained by the elders so, understood that which is lofty and excellent more than ever before.

Now, at that later time, the Exalted One was sitting in the open surrounded by the community of bhikkhus on the night of the full moon observance day of the fourth and final month of the rains, the blossoming time of the white lotus. The Exalted One surveyed the calm and silent assembly of bhikkhus, then spoke:

### THE COMMUNITY OF BHIKKHUS

"Bhikkhus, this community is not at all worthless. This community is not a failure in the least way. This community is established in the pure essence of Dhamma. Bhikkhus, this community is worthy of gifts, is worthy of hospitality, is worthy of offerings, is worthy of homage, and is a field more fertile than any other in the world for the cultivation of merit.

"Bhikkhus, this community of bhikkhus is an assembly such that people who make small offerings to it receive much and people who make large offerings receive even more. This community of bhikkhus is an assembly most difficult to find in this world. This community of bhikkhus is an assembly worthy of people packing up provisions and walking great distances to come and observe it.

"Bhikkhus, living in this community are bhikkhus who are worthy ones (arahants) without eruptions (āsavas),[24] who have lived the sublime life, have done what is to be done, have dropped all burdens, have attained their purpose, have ended the fetters to existence,[25] and are liberated through right understanding. Bhikkhus such as these are living in this community of bhikkhus.

"Bhikkhus, living in this community are bhikkhus who are non-returners through having ended the five lower fetters, who are spontaneously arisen,[26] who will realize perfect coolness in that existence

130

and by nature will never return from that world. Bhikkhus such as these are living in this community of bhikkhus.

"Bhikkhus, living in this community there are bhikkhus who are once-returners through having ended the three fetters[27] and lessened lust and hatred, who will come back to this world only once and then will put an end to *dukkha*. Bhikkhus such as these are living in this community of bhikkhus.

"Bhikkhus, living in this community are bhikkhus who are stream-enterers through having ended the three fetters, who by nature never will fall into evil again and are certain of future awakening. Bhikkhus such as these are in this community of bhikkhus.

"Bhikkhus, living in this community are bhikkhus who dwell devoted in practicing the cultivation of the four foundations of mindfulness (*satipaṭṭhāna*). Bhikkhus such as these are living in this community of bhikkhus.

"Bhikkhus, living in this community are bhikkhus who dwell devoted in practicing the cultivation of the four right efforts...[28]

...bhikkhus who dwell devoted in practicing the cultivation of the four bases of success...[29]

...bhikkhus who dwell devoted in practicing the cultivation of the five faculties...[30]

...bhikkhus who dwell devoted in practicing the cultivation of the five powers...[31]

...bhikkhus who dwell devoted in practicing the cultivation of the seven factors of awakening...[32]

...bhikkhus who dwell devoted in practicing the cultivation of the Noble Eightfold Path...[33]

...bhikkhus who dwell devoted in practicing the cultivation of friendliness (*mettā*)...

...bhikkhus who dwell devoted in practicing the cultivation of compassion (*karunā*)...

...bhikkhus who dwell devoted in practicing the cultivation of sympathetic joy (*muditā*)...

...bhikkhus who dwell devoted in practicing the cultivation of equanimity (*upekkhā*)...

...bhikkhus who dwell devoted in practicing the cultivation of the non-beautiful...[34]

...bhikkhus who dwell devoted in practicing the cultivation of the experience of impermanence (*aniccasaññā*). Bhikkhus such as these are living in this community of bhikkhus.

"Bhikkhus, living in this community are bhikkhus who dwell devoted in practicing the cultivation of mindfulness with breathing (*ānāpānasati*)."

## MINDFULNESS WITH BREATHING

"Bhikkhus, *ānāpānasati*, which one has developed and made much of, has great fruit and great benefit. *Ānāpānasati*, which one has developed and made much of, perfects the four foundations of mindfulness. The four foundations of mindfulness, which one has developed and made much of, perfect the seven factors of awakening. The seven factors of awakening, which one has developed and made much of, perfect insight knowledge and liberation.

"Bhikkhus, how does *ānāpānasati*, which one has developed and made much of, have great fruit and great benefit?

"Bhikkhus, a bhikkhu within this training (*dhamma-vinaya*), having gone into the forest, to the base of a tree or to an empty dwelling, having sat cross-legged with his body erect, securely maintains mindfulness (*sati*). Ever mindful, that bhikkhu breathes in; ever mindful, he breathes out."

### FIRST TETRAD

(1) "While breathing in long, he fully comprehends, 'I breathe in long.' While breathing out long, he fully comprehends, 'I breathe out long.'[35]

(2) "While breathing in short, he fully comprehends, 'I breathe in short.' While breathing out short, he fully comprehends, 'I breathe out short.'

(3) "He trains himself, 'Thoroughly experiencing all bodies, I shall breathe in.' He trains himself, 'Thoroughly experiencing all bodies, I shall breathe out.'[36]

(4) "He trains himself, 'Calming the body-conditioner, I shall breathe in.' He trains himself, 'Calming the body-conditioner, I shall breathe out.'"[37]

SECOND TETRAD

(5) "He trains himself, 'Thoroughly experiencing *pīti*, I shall breathe in.' He trains himself, 'Thoroughly experiencing *pīti*, I shall breathe out.'

(6) "He trains himself, 'Thoroughly experiencing *sukha*, I shall breathe in.' He trains himself, 'Thoroughly experiencing *sukha*, I shall breathe out.'

(7) "He trains himself, 'Thoroughly experiencing the mind-conditioner, I shall breathe in.' He trains himself, 'Thoroughly experiencing the mind-conditioner, I shall breathe out.'[38]

(8) "He trains himself, 'Calming the mind-conditioner, I shall breathe in.' He trains himself, 'Calming the mind-conditioner, I shall breathe out.'"[39]

THIRD TETRAD

(9) "He trains himself, 'Thoroughly experiencing the mind, I shall breathe in.' He trains himself, 'Thoroughly experiencing the mind, I shall breathe out.'[40]

(10) "He trains himself, 'Gladdening the mind, I shall breathe in.' He trains himself, 'Gladdening the mind, I shall breathe out.'[41]

(11) "He trains himself, 'Concentrating the mind, I shall breathe in.' He trains himself, 'Concentrating the mind, I shall breathe out.'[42]

(12) "He trains himself, 'Liberating the mind, I shall breathe in.' He trains himself, 'Liberating the mind, I shall breathe out.'"[43]

## FOURTH TETRAD

(13) "He trains himself, 'Constantly contemplating impermanence, I shall breathe in.' He trains himself, 'Constantly contemplating impermanence, I shall breathe out.'[44]

(14) "He trains himself, 'Constantly contemplating fading away, I shall breathe in.' He trains himself, 'Constantly contemplating fading away, I shall breathe out.'[45]

(15) "He trains himself, 'Constantly contemplating quenching, I shall breathe in.' He trains himself, 'Constantly contemplating quenching, I shall breathe out.'[46]

(16) "He trains himself, 'Constantly contemplating tossing back, I shall breathe in.' He trains himself, 'Constantly contemplating tossing back, I shall breathe out.'"[47]

"Bhikkhus, this is how *ānāpānasati*, which one has developed and made much of, has great fruit and great benefit."

### THE FOUR FOUNDATIONS OF MINDFULNESS (*SATIPAṬṬHĀNA*)

"Bhikkhus, how does *ānāpānasati*, which one has developed and made much of, perfect the four foundations of mindfulness?

"Bhikkhus, whenever a bhikkhu (1) while breathing in long fully comprehends: 'I breathe in long'; while breathing out long fully comprehends: 'I breathe out long'; or, (2) while breathing in short fully comprehends: 'I breathe in short'; while breathing out short fully comprehends: 'I breathe out short'; or, (3) trains himself: 'Thoroughly experiencing all bodies I shall breathe in…shall breathe out'; or, (4) trains himself: 'Calming the body-conditioner I shall breathe in…shall breathe out'; then that bhikkhu is considered one who lives constantly contemplating body in bodies, strives to burn up defilements, comprehends readily, and is mindful, in order to abandon all liking and disliking toward the world.[48]

"Bhikkhus, I say that the in-breaths and the out-breaths are certain bodies among all bodies. Bhikkhus, for this reason that bhikkhu is considered one who lives constantly contemplating body in bodies, strives to burn up defilements, comprehends readily, and is mindful, in order to abandon all liking and disliking toward the world.

"Bhikkhus, whenever a bhikkhu (5) trains himself: 'Thoroughly experiencing *pīti* I shall breathe in...shall breathe out'; or, (6) trains himself: 'Thoroughly experiencing *sukha* I shall breathe in...shall breathe out'; or, (7) trains himself: 'Thoroughly experiencing the mind-conditioner I shall breathe in...shall breathe out'; or, (8) trains himself: 'Calming the mind-conditioner I shall breathe in... shall breathe out'; then that bhikkhu is considered one who lives constantly contemplating feeling in feelings, strives to burn up defilements, comprehends readily, and is mindful, in order to abandon all liking and disliking toward the world.[49]

"Bhikkhus, I say that attending carefully in the mind to in-breaths and out-breaths is a certain feeling among all feelings. Bhikkhus, for this reason that bhikkhu is considered one who lives constantly contemplating feeling in feelings, strives to burn up defilements, comprehends readily, and is mindful, in order to abandon all liking and disliking toward the world.

"Bhikkhus, whenever a bhikkhu (9) trains himself: 'Thoroughly experiencing the mind I shall breathe in...shall breathe out'; or, (10) trains himself: 'Gladdening the mind I shall breathe in...shall breathe out'; or, (11) trains himself: 'Concentrating the mind I shall breathe in...shall breathe out'; or, (12) trains himself: 'Liberating the mind I shall breathe in...shall breathe out'; then that bhikkhu is considered one who lives constantly contemplating mind in the mind, strives to burn up defilements, comprehends readily, and is mindful, in order to abandon all liking and disliking toward the world.[50]

"Bhikkhus, I do not say that *ānāpānasati* is possible for a person who has straying mindfulness and lacks ready comprehension. Bhikkhus, for this reason that bhikkhu is considered one who lives constantly contemplating mind in the mind, strives to burn up defilements, comprehends readily, and is mindful, in order to abandon all liking and disliking toward the world.

"Bhikkhus, whenever a bhikkhu (13) trains himself: 'Constantly contemplating impermanence I shall breathe in...shall breathe out'; or, (14) trains himself: 'Constantly contemplating fading away I shall breathe in...shall breathe out'; or, (15) trains himself: 'Constantly contemplating quenching I shall breathe in…shall breathe out'; or, (16) trains himself: 'Constantly contemplating tossing back I shall breathe in…shall breathe out'; then that bhikkhu is considered one who lives constantly contemplating Dhamma in *dhammas*, strives to burn up defilements, comprehends readily, and is mindful, in order to abandon all liking and disliking toward the world.[51]

"That bhikkhu looks on with perfect equanimity because he has seen with wisdom the abandoning of all liking and disliking toward the world. Bhikkhus, for this reason that bhikkhu is considered one who lives constantly contemplating Dhamma in *dhammas*, strives to burn up defilements, comprehends readily, and is mindful, in order to abandon all liking and disliking toward the world.

"Bhikkhus, this is how *ānāpānasati*, which one has developed and made much of, perfects the four foundations of mindfulness."

## THE SEVEN FACTORS OF AWAKENING (*BOJJHAṄGA*)

"Bhikkhus, how do the four foundations of mindfulness, which one has developed and made much of, perfect the seven factors of awakening?

"Bhikkhus, whenever a bhikkhu is one who lives constantly contemplating body in bodies[52]…is one who lives constantly contemplating feeling in feelings…is one who lives constantly contemplating mind in the mind…is one who lives constantly contemplating Dhamma in *dhammas*, strives to burn up defilements, comprehends readily, and is mindful, in order to abandon all liking and disliking toward the world; then the *sati* of that bhikkhu thus established is natural and unconfused.

"Bhikkhus, whenever the *sati* of that bhikkhu thus established is natural and unconfused, then the mindfulness enlightenment factor (*sati-sambojjhaṅga*) is engaged by that bhikkhu; he develops it further and finally its development in him is perfected. That bhikkhu, when mindful in such a way, selects, takes up, and scrutinizes these *dhammas* with wisdom.

"Bhikkhus, whenever a bhikkhu is mindful in such a way, selects, takes up, and scrutinizes these *dhammas* with wisdom; then the investigation of the *dhammas'* factor of awakening (*dhamma-vicaya-sambojjhaṅga*) is engaged by that bhikkhu; he develops it further and finally its development in him is perfected. When that bhikkhu selects, takes up, and scrutinizes these *dhammas* with wisdom, unwavering effort is engaged by him.

"Bhikkhus, whenever unwavering energy is engaged by a bhikkhu who selects, takes up, and scrutinizes these *dhammas* with wisdom; then the energy factor of awakening (*viriya-sambojjhanga*) is engaged by him; he develops it further and its development in him is perfected. When energy is engaged by that bhikkhu, non-sensual *piti* arises.[53]

"Bhikkhus, whenever non-sensual *piti* arises in the bhikkhu who has engaged energy, then the contentment factor of awakening (*piti-sambojjhanga*) is engaged by that bhikkhu; he develops it further and its development in him is perfected. When that bhikkhu's mind is contented, both body is calmed and mind is calmed.

"Bhikkhus, whenever both the body and the mind of a bhikkhu who is contented are calm, then the tranquility factor of awakening (*passaddhi-sambojjhanga*) is engaged by him; he develops it further and its development in him is perfected. When that bhikkhu's body is calmed, there is joy and the mind becomes concentrated.

"Bhikkhus, whenever the mind of a bhikkhu whose body is calmed and who is joyful becomes concentrated, then the concentration factor of awakening (*samadhi-sambojjhanga*) is engaged by that bhikkhu; he develops it further and its development in him is perfected. That bhikkhu looks upon that concentrated mind with perfect equanimity.

"Bhikkhus, whenever a bhikkhu looks upon that concentrated mind with perfect equanimity, then the equanimity factor of awakening (*upekkha-sambojjhanga*) is engaged by that bhikkhu; he develops it further and its development in him is perfected.

"Bhikkhus, this is how the four foundations of mindfulness, which one has developed and made much of, perfect the seven factors of awakening."[54]

### KNOWLEDGE AND LIBERATION

"Bhikkhus, how do the seven factors of awakening, which one has developed and made much of, perfect knowledge (*vijja*) and liberation (*vimutti*)?

"Bhikkhus, a bhikkhu in this training develops *sati-sambojjhaṅga*, which depends on *viveka* (solitude, aloneness), which depends on *virāga* (fading away), which depends on *nirodhā* (quenching), which leads to *vossagga* (dropping away, letting go).[55]

"He develops *dhammavicaya-sambojjhaṅga*, which depends on *viveka*, on *virāga*, on *nirodhā*, and leads to *vossagga*.

"He develops *viriya sambojjhaṅga*, which depends on *viveka*, on *virāga*, on *nirodhā*, and leads to *vossagga*.

"He develops *pīti-sambojjhaṅga*, which depends on *viveka*, on *virāga*, on *nirodhā*, and leads to *vossagga*.

"He develops *passaddhi-sambojjhaṅga*, which depends on *viveka*, on *virāga*, on *nirodhā*, and leads to *vossagga*.

"He develops *samādhi-sambojjhaṅga*, which depends on *viveka*, on *virāga*, on *nirodhā*, and leads to *vossagga*.

"He develops *upekkhā-sambojjhaṅga*, which depends on *viveka*, on *virāga*, on *nirodhā*, and leads to *vossagga*.

"Bhikkhus, this is how the seven factors of awakening, which one has developed and made much of, perfect knowledge and liberation."[56]

After the Exalted One had spoken, the bhikkhus were contented and rejoiced at the Exalted One's words.

# Notes

1. In some contexts, *dhamma* merely means "thing"; in this instance, we do not capitalize it. However, when *Dhamma* refers to "the secret of nature for developing life," then to distinguish it from *dhamma* as "thing," we have capitalized it.

2. The Thai word *kuab-kum* is used throughout this book. It can be translated "to regulate; to control or confine; to master; to oversee, supervise, or superintend." When one of these translations appear, all of the rest should be understood. In all cases, *kuab-kum* depends on *sati* and wisdom, never on force or willpower.

3. The *wat* is the traditional place for Thai travelers to rest and sleep, but nowadays it is no longer used by merchants and government employees, who prefer hotels with their modern amenities.

4. At Suan Mokkh, to the right and past the *hin kong*, where Ajahn Buddhadāsa lectured, this theater is one of the many vehicles for sharing Dhamma. It not only contains relief sculptures copied from the oldest Buddhist shrines in India that tell the life of the Buddha but also many Dhamma paintings from various Buddhist traditions.

5. The fundamental dualism that distracts us from the middle way and causes us to become caught up in attachment, selfishness, and *dukkha*.

6. Even those who use kneelers and chairs must strive to follow these principles: stability, weight evenly distributed, and spine straight.

7. The *ānāpānasati* form of *prāṇāyāma* is not an overt or forced "control" of the breath. It is a subtle and patient guide or regulator, a feather rather than a hammer.

8. However, this is not yet the highest degree of control.

9. See chapter four.

10. The *hin kong* lecture area is covered by sand and is full of trees, rocks, and boulders. It is to these boulders that Ajahn Buddhadāsa refers here.

11. See Ajahn Buddhadāsa's *Practical Dependent Origination* (Bangkok: The Dhamma Study and Practice Group, 1992) and forthcoming translations on the subject. See also P. A. Payutto, *Dependent Origination: The Buddhist Law of Conditionality* (Bangkok: Buddha-Dhamma Foundation, 1994).

12. The reader can find a full translation of this sutta on pp. 113–122.

13. *Dhammapada*, 184.

14. The *Mahāsatipaṭṭhāna Sutta* (D.ii.22) and the somewhat shorter *Satipaṭṭhāna Sutta* (M.i.10), which follows the same pattern as the *Mahā* but is less detailed and extensive.

15. Whether these methods are correct and useful, or not, is not at issue here.

16. These quoted paragraphs are from a retreat talk given by Ajahn Buddhadāsa on 5 April 1987.

17. Ibid.

18. From a retreat talk given by Ajahn Buddhadāsa on 5 May 1987.

19. From the talk of 5 April 1987.

20. The translator is not well-versed in Pali. This rendering is based on Ajahn Buddhadāsa's translation from Pali to Thai and his line-by-line explanation of that translation. Previous English translations by I. B. Horner, Bhikkhu Ñāṇamoli, and Bhikkhu Nāgasena have been consulted as well.

21. *Bhagavā*, a frequent epithet of the Buddha, was a common form of address in India. Buddhists, however, reserve it for the Buddha. It is often translated as "Blessed One."

22. Then the capital of the kingdom of Kosala, which was located between the Himalayas and the Ganges River, Sāvatthi was the geographical center of the Buddha's teaching during his lifetime. He spent twenty-five of forty-five rains residences there.

23. The third month of the four-month-long rainy season.

24. Conditions that ferment in and flow out or erupt from the mind's depths. Usually given as three: *kāmāsava*, eruption of sensuality; *bhavāsava*, eruption of becoming; and *avijjāsava*, eruption of igno-

rance. Sometimes a fourth is added: *diṭṭhāsava*, eruption of views. The ending of the *āsāvas* is synonymous with perfect awakening. (Other translations are "cankers, taints, influxes.")

25. The ten *saṁyojana* that bind beings to the cycles of becoming are personality belief, uncertainty about the path, superstitious use of rituals and practices, sensuous lust, ill will, lust for fine material existence, lust for immaterial existence, conceit, restlessness, and ignorance.

26. *Oppātika*, born instantly and fully mature without going through the process of conception, gestation, infancy, and childhood—that is, instantaneous mental birth (not necessarily "rebirth" in the conventional sense).

27. The first three of the ten *saṁyojana*.

28. The four *sammappadhāna* are: (1) the effort to prevent or avoid unwholesome states that have not arisen; (2) the effort to overcome or abandon unwholesome states that have arisen; (3) the effort to develop wholesome states that have not arisen; and (4) the effort to maintain wholesome states that have arisen.

29. The four *iddhipāda* are: *chanda*, love of duty; *viriya*, effort in duty; *citta*, thoughtfulness regarding duty; and *vimaṁsā*, investigation of duty through practicing Dhamma.

30. The five *indriya* are: *saddhā*, confidence, faith; *viriya*, effort, energy; *sati*, mindfulness; *samādhi*, concentration; and *paññā*, wisdom.

31. The five *bala* have the same names as the five *indriya*, but function differently. The five *bala* function as powers that provide the strength needed to overcome and withstand their opposites (i.e., lack of confidence, laziness, carelessness, distraction, and delusion.) The five *indriya* are the chief sovereign or controlling faculties that lead each group of *dhammas* as they deal with their opposites (e.g., lack of confidence).

32. The seven *bojjhanga* are: *sati*, mindfulness; *dhammavicaya*, investigation of dhamma; *viriya*, effort; *pīti*, contentment; *passaddhi*, tranquility; *samādhi*, concentration; and *upekkhā*, equanimity. They are discussed in detail later in the *Sutta*.

33. The *ariya-aṭṭhaṅgika-magga* consists of right understanding, right aspiration, right speech, right action, right livelihood, right effort, right mindfulness, and right concentration.

34. *Asubha-bhāvanā* is used to counteract and overcome lust.

35. The words "fully comprehends" mean that there is *sati-sampajañña* (mindfulness and ready comprehension) with every moment of noting the in-breaths and out-breaths in all their aspects.

36. "Bodies" (*kāya*) refers to the breath in its aspect of conditioning the flesh-body. "Experiencing all bodies" *(sabbakāyaṁ paṭisaṁvetī)* refers to directly knowing the breath's characteristics—such as short or long, coarse or fine, calm or agitated—knowing how it conditions the flesh-body, knowing its natural processes of change, and knowing other relevant details about the breathing.

37. As the breath is calmed and refined, the conditioning of the body is calmed, and the mind becomes calm and concentrated to the extent, finally, of *jhāna*.

38. Know how feelings (*vedanā*), especially the pleasant ones, condition the mind with every breath.

39. Be able to decrease the ability of the feelings to condition the mind. Decrease their conditioning of the mind until there is nothing that is conditioning it, that is, there is no feeling, no perception (*saññā*), and no thought (*vitakka*) at that time.

40. Know the exact state of mind at that moment, whether it is spotless or darkened, calm or agitated, prepared to work (contemplate Dhamma) or not ready, or whatever state may arise.

41. Be able to amuse the mind with Dhamma in various ways.

42. Expertly observe the qualities and extent of the mind's *samādhi*.

43. Observe the qualities and extent of the mind's freedom from attachment.

44. With every breath, use the correctly concentrated mind to contemplate impermanence continuously, until realizing the unsatisfactoriness, selflessness, voidness, and thusness of all conditioned things.

45. With every breath, examine the state of the mind being disenchanted with, weary of, and dispassionate toward the things it has desired and grasped.

46. Examine the ceasing of attachment and realize it as being *nibbāna*, the ceasing and quenching of *dukkha*, then cherish it as the mind's regular object.

47. Realize that all conditioned things have been freed from attachment. This condition arises in the moments of path (*magga*) and path fruition (*phala*).

48. "Contemplating body in bodies" means seeing the truth of bodies directly within bodies themselves and seeing all the components of the body as being small bodies within the collective body. The breath is one body. It conditions all kinds of bodies, whether physical or mental, beginning with the flesh-body up to the joy of *jhāna*. Contemplate these bodies until there is no more attachment to any of them.

49. Contemplate feelings in the same way that bodies have been contemplated. Contemplate *pīti* and *sukha* until there is no attachment to any feelings anywhere.

50. Contemplate the mind in the same way as bodies and feelings were contemplated, until there is no attachment to any mind states.

51. Contemplate the truth of Dhamma in all things (*dhammas*) until there is no attachment left to any *dhamma*, from the lowest to the highest, including *nibbāna*.

52. The original Pali explains how all seven factors can develop upon each one of the four foundations of mindfulness, with each foundation considered separately. Here, for the sake of brevity, we have grouped all four foundations together.

53. This *pīti* is pure and associated with Dhamma; it has nothing to do with the physical senses. Such *pīti* occurs during *jhāna* and while realizing Dhamma.

54. The *bojjhaṅga* develop as follows. Mindfulness fixes on a specific thing, and investigation of *dhammas* examines it in detail, with energy and effort, until contentment arises. Then, the mind calms until it becomes tranquil and is concentrated in contemplating the object. Equanimity firmly and unwaveringly watches over and guards that concentration, and the penetration of and awakening to Dhamma continues by itself until complete.

55. Here *vossagga* means no longer becoming attached to previous objects of attachment, because the mind is disenchanted with them and now inclines toward the quenching of *dukkha*, namely, *nibbāna*. *Viveka, virāga, nirodha*, and *vossagga* are synonyms of *nibbāna*.

56. *Vijjā* is the insight knowledge of the path (*magga-ñāṇa*) that follows upon the insights experienced through the practice of ānāpānasati. Its function is to penetrate thoroughly and destroy ignorance (*avijjā*). *Vimutti* is insight knowledge of fruition (*phala-ñāṇa*), the result of the path having done its work of clearing away *avijjā*. It is the mind's direct experience of being liberated from *dukkha*.

# Glossary

AN ABUNDANCE OF PALI TERMS are used in this manual. This reflects Ajahn Buddhadāsa's advice that sincere student-practitioners of Buddhism should be familiar with the most important Pali terms and their correct meanings, for they offer a precision, clarity, and depth that English equivalents may lack. Most of the terms used here are explained within the text. This glossary is provided for easy reference and additional information. We also include some key English terms so that they may be checked with their Pali equivalents. As we have followed Ajahn Buddhadāsa's explanations, some of the translations and definitions found here may differ from those found in other books. Thus, to make the most of this manual, you need to understand how Ajahn Buddhadāsa uses these terms. Even those who have studied Pali may find some helpful insights here.

Both Pali and English terms are listed in alphabetical order according to the English language. Pali terms are defined and explained. When appropriate, we cite textual passages in which specific terms are discussed. Spelling is according to standard Thai usage (see *Dictionary of Buddhism*, Phra Rājavoramuni [P. A. Payutto], Bangkok: Mahāculalongkorn Rājavidayālai, 1985). English terms are not defined. You can find their meaning under the given Pali equivalent. In any case, it is important that you be wary of English terms found here and elsewhere. They seldom correspond exactly to the Pali terms they are meant to translate, and they often carry inappropriate connotations. It is always best to learn the Pali terms and their proper meanings. Terms that appear only once or are of minor importance may not be included in this glossary. All Pali terms used in the explanations below are themselves also explained in their own glossary entries.

*Ācariya*. Teacher, master.

*Ādīnava*. Penalty, disadvantage, peril, harm: the hook within the bait (*assāda*); the lowly, harmful, negative, or wicked aspect of something.

*Āna*. In-breath, inhalation, breathing in. The corresponding verb is *assasati*, to breathe in.

*Ānāpānasati.* Mindfulness with breathing in and out: to note, investigate, and contemplate a *dhamma* (thing, fact, truth) while being mindful of every in-breath and out-breath. In the Buddha's complete system of *ānāpānasati*, a natural progression of sixteen lessons or *dhammas* are practiced in order to explore fully the *satipaṭṭhāna* and realize liberation.

*Anattā, anattatā.* Not-self, selflessness, non-selfhood: the fact that all things without exception, including *nibbāna*, are not-self and lack any essence or substance that could properly be called a "self." This truth does not deny the existence of "things" (see *dhamma*) but denies that they can be owned or controlled or be an owner or controller in any but a relative, conventional sense. *Anattā* is the third fundamental characteristic of *sankhāra*. *Anattā* is an inevitable result of *aniccaṁ*. All things are what they are and are not-self. *Anattā* is more or less a synonym of *suññatā*.

*Aniccaṁ, anicca, aniccatā.* Impermanence, instability, flux: conditioned things are ever-changing, in ceaseless transformation, and constantly arising, manifesting, and extinguishing. All concocted things decay and pass away. This is the first fundamental characteristic of *sankhāra*.

*Anupassanā.* Contemplation: sustained, nonverbal, nonreactive, uninvolved, even-minded scrutiny of a *dhamma*, the essence of meditation. The four *satipaṭṭhāna* are the necessary objects of contemplation, thus: *kāyānupassanā*, contemplation of body, *vedanānupassanā*, contemplation of feeling, *cittānupassanā*, contemplation of mind, *dhammānupassanā*, contemplation of Dhamma. True *anupassanā* arises from *vipassanā* (insight).

*Apāna.* Out-breath, exhalation, breathing out. The verb form is *passasati*, to breathe out.

*Arahant.* Worthy one, fully awakened being, perfected human being: a living being completely free and void of all attachment, *kilesa*, self-belief, selfishness, danger, and *dukkha*. To speak of such a one in terms of entering *nibbāna* or not, as is done in Mahāyāna polemics, is a misunderstanding of the Buddha's teaching.

*Ariya-sacca.* Noble truths: there are four that together are one truth, namely: *dukkha*, the cause of *dukkha*, which is craving, the end of *dukkha*, which occurs when craving ends, and the path of practice that leads to the end of *dukkha*. The *arahant*, the truly enlightened being, has penetrated these truths thoroughly.

*Assāda.* Bait, charm, attractiveness: the tasty morsel hiding the hook (*ādīnava*): the lovely, satisfying, infatuating, positive quality of something.

*Attā.* Self, ego, (Sanskrit, *atman*): the instinctual feeling and illusion (mental concoction) that there is some personal, separate "I" in life. Although theories about self abound, all are mere speculation about something that exists only in our imagination. In a conventional sense, the *attā* can be a useful concept, belief, or perception, but it ultimately has no validity. That conventional "self" is not-self (*anattā*). No individual, independent, inherently self-existing, free-willing substance can be found anywhere, whether within or without human life (the five *khandhas*) and experience.

Attachment. *Upādāna.*

*Avijjā.* Not-knowing, ignorance, wrong knowledge, foolishness: the lack, partial or total, of *vijjā* (correct knowledge). *Avijjā* has two levels: the lack of knowledge that comes with birth, and the wrong knowledge conditioned and accumulated later.

*Āyatana.* Sense media, connecters: there are two aspects or sets of *āyatana*, internal and external. The internal *āyatana* are the eyes, ears, nose, tongue, body, and mind (mental-sense): that is, the six sense doors, the sense organs, and their corresponding portions of the nervous system. The external *āyatana* are forms, sounds, smells, tastes, touches, and mental-concerns: that is, the concerns or objects of sensory experience. *Nibbāna* is described as an *āyatana*, an unconditioned *āyatana*.

*Bhāvanā.* Development, cultivation, meditation: to produce or make happen. In particular, to cultivate skillful, wholesome qualities of mind. The term *citta-bhāvanā* (mental development) is preferable to the vague and often confusing "meditation." The Buddha mentioned four *bhāvanā*: *kāya, sīla, citta,* and *paññā*.

Body. *Kāya.*

*Bojjhaṅga.* Factors of awakening, enlightenment factors: these seven mental factors must be perfected, in succession, for the mind to be liberated. First, *sati* (mindfulness) fixes on a certain *dhamma*. Then, *dhamma-vicaya* (analysis of *dhamma*) investigates that thing subtly, precisely, and profoundly. Next, *viriya* (effort, energy) arises, which leads to *pīti* (contentment). Then, the mind develops *passaddhi* (tranquility) because of that contentment, such that there is *samādhi* (concentration) in the contemplation of that *dhamma*. Lastly, *samādhi* is continuously and evenly guarded by *upekkhā* (equanimity) as the truth of that *dhamma* and all Dhamma is penetrated and realized.

*Buddha.* The Knowing, Awakened, Fully Blossomed One, especially the Perfectly Self-Awakened One (*sammāsambuddha*). Specifically, Buddha refers to the historical prophet under whom Buddhism was founded, otherwise referred to as *Bhāgavā* (Blessed One) by followers and Samana Gotama by others. Generally, any arahant is also a buddha, that is, one who is awakened from ignorance and the sleep of egoism. Finally, a buddha is the ultimate potential of all human beings. The primary qualities (*guṭa*) of a buddha are wisdom, purity, and compassion.

*Citta.* Mind, heart, consciousness: all aspects, qualities, and functions of the living being that are not material-physical. In a more limited sense, *citta* is the consciousness-potential when it "thinks." *Citta* is also used to name that which is defiled by *kilesa* and realizes *nibbāna*. Further, *citta* is the maker of *kamma* or doer of actions and receives the fruits of those actions; that is, *citta* is the creator of all that we do and experience. *Citta* requires a physical structure, the body, and functions together with it. (Compare with *mano* and *viññāṭa*.)

*Citta-sankhāra.* Mind-conditioner: the *vedanā* that conditions and concocts the *citta*.

Concentration. *Samādhi*, calm-collectedness.

Craving. *taṇhā*, foolish desire, blind want.

Defilement. *Kilesa*: namely, greed, hatred, and delusion.

*dhamma.* Thing, nature, things: both conditioned phenomena and unconditioned noumenon.

*Dhamma* (Sanskrit, *Dharma*). Truth, nature, law, order, duty: the secret of nature which must be understood in order to develop life to the highest possible purpose and benefit. The four primary meanings of *Dhamma* are nature, the law and truth of nature, the duty to be performed in accordance with natural law, and the results or benefits that arise from the performance of that duty.

*Dhamma-jāti.* Nature: that which exists within itself, by itself, of itself, and as its own law. *Dhamma-jāti* encompasses all things, both human and non-human.

*Dosa.* Hatred, ill-will: the second category of *kilesa*; includes anger, aversion, dislike, and all other negative thoughts and emotions; characterized by the mind pushing away an object.

*Dukkha, dukkhaṁ.* Stress, suffering, misery, unsatisfactoriness, pain: literally, "hard to endure, difficult to bear." In its limited sense, *dukkha* is the quality of experience that results when the mind is conditioned by *avijjā* into craving, attachment, egoism, and selfishness. This feeling takes on forms such as disappointment, dissatisfaction, frustration, agitation, anguish, dis-ease, despair—from the crudest to the subtlest levels. In its universal sense, *dukkhaṁ* is the inherent condition of unsatisfactoriness, ugliness, and misery in all impermanent, conditioned things (*sankhāra*). This second fundamental characteristic is the result of *aniccaṁ*: impermanent things cannot satisfy our wants and desires no matter how hard we try (and cry). The inherent decay and dissolution of things is misery.

Ego. *Attā.*

*Ekaggatā.* One-pointedness: to have a single peak, focus, or pinnacle. The state in which the flow of mental energy is gathered and focused on a single object, especially an exalted one, such as *nibbāna.*

Emancipation. *Vimutti.*

Feeling. *Vedanā*, feelings. (Note: Sometimes the word "feeling" can denote other things that are not *vedanā*, such as "mood, emotion, or tactile sensation.")

*Idappaccayatā.* The law of conditionality (or causality), the law of nature: literally, "the state of having this as condition." All natural laws can be seen in *idappaccayatā*. Because all creation, preservation, and destruction occurs through this law, it can be called the "Buddhist God."

*Jhāna.* Peering, contemplation, absorption, meditation: one-pointed focus of the mind on an object, for the purpose of developing tranquility, or on impermanence, for the purpose of developing insight. *Jhāna* is understood as both an activity of the mind (focusing, peering, looking intently and deeply) and the results of that activity. These results are of two types: (1) the *rūpajhānas*, the *jhānas* dependent on the forms of material objects, mental absorption into objects of finer materiality; and (2) the *arūpajhānas*, the *jhānas* dependent on immaterial or formless objects. The *jhānas* are listed below. The first four are the *rūpajhānas*, and the second four are the *arūpajhānas*.

*paṭhama-jhāna*, which has five factors: noting (the object), experiencing (the object), rapture, joy, and one-pointedness.

*dutiya-jhāna*, which has three factors: rapture, joy, and one-pointedness.

*tatiya-jhāna*, which has two factors: joy and one-pointedness.

*catuttha-jhāna*, which has two factors: equanimity and one-pointedness.

*ākāsānañcāyatana*, which is the experience of infinite space.

*viññāṭañcāyatana*, which is the experience of infinite consciousness.

*ākiñcaññāyatana*, which is the experience of infinite nothingness.

*nevasaññānāsannāyatana*, which is the experience that is neither-experience-nor-nonexperience.

These eight levels of successively more refined *samādhi* are very useful but are not necessary for the successful practice of *ānāpānasati*.

*Jhānaṅga.* Factors of *jhāna*: the functions or qualities of mind that exist within *jhāna*. In the first *jhāna* there are five factors: *vitakka*, noting the object or *nimitta*; *vicāra*, experiencing the object; *pīti*, rapture, contentment; *sukha*, joy; and *ekaggatā*, one-pointedness. The other *jhāna* have successively fewer factors. (See *jhāna*.)

*Kalyāna-mitta.* Good friend, noble companion: a spiritual guide and advisor.

*Kāma.* Sensuality, sexuality: strong desire and its objects. Seeking and indulging in sensual pleasures; not to be confused with *kamma*.

*Kamma* (Sanskrit, *karma*). Action: actions of body, speech, and mind arising from wholesome and unwholesome volitions. Good intentions and actions bring good results; bad intentions and actions bring bad results. Unintentional actions are not *kamma*, are not Dhammically significant. *Kamma* has nothing to do with fate, luck, or fortune, nor does it mean the result of *kamma*.

*Kāya.* Body, group, collection, heap, squad: something composed of various elements, organs, or parts. Generally used for the physical body; refers to either the whole body or its parts ("breath-body" and "flesh-body").

*Kāya-sankhāra.* Body-conditioner: the breath, which conditions and influences the body directly. (Also can be translated "body-condition.")

*Khandha.* Aggregates, groups, heaps, categories: the five basic functions that constitute a human life. These groups are not entities in themselves; they are merely the categories into which all aspects of our lives can be analyzed (except *nibbāna*). None of them are a "self," nor do they have anything to do with selfhood, nor is there any "self" apart from them. The five are *rūpa-khandha*, form aggregate (corporeality);

*vedanā-khandha,* feeling aggregate; *saññā-khandha,* perception aggregate (including memory, recognition, discrimination, evaluation); *sankhāra-khandha,* thought aggregate (including emotion); and *viññāta-khandha,* sense consciousness aggregate. When they become the basis for attachment, the five become the *upādāna-khandha.*

*Kilesa.* Defilements, impurities: all the things that dull, darken, dirty, defile, agitate, stress, and sadden the *citta.* The three categories of *kilesa* are *lobha, dosa,* and *moha.*

*Lobha.* Greed: the first category of *kilesa;* includes erotic love, lust, miserliness, and all other "positive" thoughts and emotions; characterized by the mind pulling in an object. See *rāga.*

*Loka.* World: that which must break, shatter, and disintegrate.

*Lokiya.* Worldly, mundane, worldly conditions: to be trapped within and beneath the world; to be of the world.

*Lokuttara.* Transcendent, above and beyond the world, supramundane: to be free of worldly conditions although living in the world.

Lust. *Rāga.*

*Magga.* Path, way: the Noble Eightfold Path, the middle way out of all *dukkha.*

*Magga-phala-nibbāna.* Path, fruition, and *nibbāna:* this compound refers to the three activities that occur in rapid succession in the realization of Dhamma. *Magga* (path) is the activity of *vipassanā* cutting through defilements. *Phala* (fruit) is the successful completion of that cutting, the result of *magga. Nibbāna* is the coolness that appears once the defilements are cut. (Although these three terms appear separately throughout the Pali texts and are commonly grouped in the commentaries, their compound is found only in Thai.)

*Mahaggatā.* Superiority, great-mindedness: a superior, better than usual state (of mind).

*Mano.* Mind-sense, mind: the name given to the consciousness-element when it feels, experiences, knows, and is aware; mind as inner *āyatana* (sense organ). (Compare with *citta* and *viññāta.*)

*Māra.* Tempter, demon, devil; literally, "killer of goodness": often personified, the real tempters and murderers are the defilements.

Mind. *Citta* or *mano* or "*viññāṭa*," depending on the aspect referred to.

Mindfulness. *Sati.*

*Moha.* Delusion: the third category of *kilesa*; includes stupidity, fear, worry, confusion, doubt, envy, infatuation, hope, and expectation; characterized by the mind spinning around its object.

*Nibbāna.* Coolness: the ultimate goal of Buddhist practice and the highest achievement of humanity, beyond birth and death, good and evil. *Nibbāna* manifests fully when the fires of *kilesa*, attachment, selfishness, and *dukkha* are completely and finally quenched. *Nibbāna* is to be realized in this lifetime and should never be confused with death.

*Nibbuto.* Coolness, one who is cooled: a coolness that occurs when, either spontaneously or through correct Dhamma practice, the *kilesa* subside temporarily. *Sāmāyika-nibbāna* (temporary coolness) and *tadaṅga-nibbāna* (coincidental coolness) are types of *nibbuto*.

*Nimitta.* Image, sign, imaginary object: in the context of *ānāpānasati* practice, *nimitta* refers to a mentally created image that arises out of concentration upon the guarding point and that is used to develop *samādhi* further in step four. There are three stages: the initial image; images manipulated as a training exercise; and the final image, which is neutral, refined, and soothing, and used as a basis for *jhāna*.

*Nirodhā.* Quenching, cessation, extinction: a synonym for *nibbāna*, the end of attachment and *dukkha*. In Buddhism, *nirodhā* always refers to the cessation of ignorance, clinging, and *dukkha*, not to the death of the human being. The lesson of step fifteen.

*Nivaraṭa.* Hindrances, obstacles: semi-defilements that get in the way of success in any endeavor, especially mental development. The five hindrances are *kāmachandha*, sensuousness; *vyāpāda*, aversion: *thīnamiddha*, sloth and torpor; *uddhacca-kukkucca*, restlessness and agitation; and *vicikicchā*, doubt. (Do not confuse *nivaraṭa* with *nirvāna*, the Sanskrit *nibbāna*.)

*Paññā.* Wisdom, insight, intuitive wisdom: correct understanding of the truth needed to quench *dukkha*. *Paññā* is the third *sikkhā* (training) and the beginning of the Noble Eightfold Path. *Paññā* (rather than faith or willpower) is the characteristic quality of Buddhism.

*Paṭicca-samuppāda.* Dependent co-origination, conditioned co-arising: the profound and detailed causal succession, and its description, that concocts *dukkha*. Because of ignorance (*avijjā*), there is concocting (*sankhāra*); because of concocting, there is sense consciousness (*viññāta*); because of sense consciousness there is mind and body (*nāma-rūpa*); because of mind and body there is sense-media (*salāyatana*); because of sense-media there is sense-contact (*phassa*); because of sense-contact there is feeling (*vedanā*); because of feeling there is craving (*taṇhā*); because of craving there is attachment (*upādāna*); because of attachment there is becoming (*bhava*); because of becoming there is birth (*jāti*); because of birth, there is aging and death (*jāra-mārata*); and thus arises the entire mass of *dukkha*.

*Paṭinissagga*. Throwing back, giving up, relinquishment: to stop claiming things as "I" and "mine," and return them to Dhamma-Nature. The lesson of step sixteen.

*Phassa*. Contact, sense experience: the meeting and working together of inner *āyatana*, outer *āyatana*, and the *viññāna* dependent on them: for example, eye, form, and eye-consciousness. There is *phassa* when a sensual stimulus has a sufficient impact upon the mind to draw a response, either positive or negative, beginning with *vedanā*. There are six kinds of *phassa* corresponding to the six senses.

*Pīti*. Contentment, satisfaction, rapture: the excited happiness (pleasant *vedanā*) that arises when one is successful in something. *Pīti* is the lesson of step five.

*Prana* (Sanskrit), *pana* (Pali). Breath, life force, life: that which sustains and nurtures life.

*Praṇāyāma* (Sanskrit). Control of the *praṇa*, breath control.

*Rāga*. Lust: desire to get or have. *Rāga* can be sexual or sensual, material, and immaterial, depending on its object. (See *lobha*.)

*Sacca*. Truth.

*Sacca-dhamma*. Truth, fact, reality.

*Samādhi*. Concentration, collectedness, mental calmness and stability: the gathering together, focusing, and integration of the mental flow. Proper *samādhi* has the qualities of purity, clarity, stability, strength, readiness, flexibility, and gentleness. It is perfected in *ekaggatā* and *jhāna*. The supreme *samādhi* is the one-pointed mind with *nibbāna* as its sole concern or object. *Samādhi* is the second *sikkhā*.

*Sampajañña.* Wisdom-in-action, ready comprehension, clear comprehension: the specific application of *paññā* as required in a given situation.

*Sangha.* Community: the community of the Buddha's followers who practice thoroughly, directly, insightfully, and correctly. *Sangha* includes lay women, lay men, nuns, and monks.

*Sankhāra.* Conditioned thing, concoction, phenomenon, formation: anything depends on other things or conditions for its existence. There are three aspects of *sankhāra*: concocter, conditioner, the cause of conditioning; concoction, condition, the result of conditioning; and the activity or process of concocting and conditioning.

*Santi.* Peace, spiritual tranquility.

*Sāsanā.* Religion: the behavior and practice that binds the human being to the supreme entity (whatever we name it).

*Sati.* Mindfulness, recollection, reflective awareness: the mind's ability to recall, know, and contemplate itself. *Sati* is the vehicle or transport mechanism for *paññā*; without *sati*, wisdom cannot be developed, retrieved, or applied. *Sati* is not memory, although the two are related. Nor is it mere heedfulness or carefulness. *Sati* allows us to be aware of what we are about to do. It is characterized by speed and agility.

*Satipaṭṭhāna.* Foundations or applications of mindfulness: the four bases to which *sati* must be applied in mental development. Life is investigated through these four subjects of spiritual study: *kāya, vedanā, citta,* and Dhamma.

*Sikkhā.* Training: the three aspects of the one path, of the middle way. All Buddhist practices fit within the three *sikkhā*: *sīla, samādhi,* and *paññā*.

*Sīla.* Morality, virtue, normality: verbal and bodily action in accordance with Dhamma. Much more than following rules or precepts, true *sīla* comes with wisdom and is undertaken joyfully; its essence is nonharming of others and oneself. The first *sikkhā*.

*Sukha.* Joy, happiness, bliss: literally, "easy to bear"; tranquil, soothing, pleasant *vedanā*. *Sukha* results from *pīti*, which stimulates, and is the lesson of step six.

*Suññatā.* Voidness, emptiness: the state of being void and free of selfhood, soul, ego, or anything that could be taken to be "I" or "mine"; also, the state of being void and free of defilement.

*Taṇhā.* Craving, blind want, foolish desire: the cause of *dukkha* (second *ariya-sacca*), not to be confused with "wise want" (*sammā-sankappa*, right aspiration). *Taṇhā* is conditioned by foolish *vedanā* and, in turn, concocts *upādāna.*

*Tathatā.* Thusness, suchness, just-like-thatness: neither this nor that, the reality of non-duality. Things are just as they are (impermanent, unsatisfactory, and not-self) regardless of our likes and dislikes, suppositions and beliefs, hopes and memories.

*Upādāna.* Attachment, clinging, grasping: to hold onto something foolishly, to regard things as "I" and "mine," to take things personally.

*Vedanā.* Feeling, sensation: the mental quality that colors sense experiences (*phassa*). There are three kinds: *sukha-vedanā*, pleasant, nice, agreeable, delicious feeling; *dukkha-vedanā*, unpleasant, disagreeable, painful feeling; and *adukkhamassukha-vedanā*, neither-unpleasant-nor-pleasant, indeterminate feeling. *Vedanā* is conditioned by *phassa* (sense contact). If *vedanā* arises through ignorance, it will concoct craving. If *vedanā* arises with wisdom, it will be harmless or beneficial. This subtle activity of mind (not physical sensation) is not emotion, nor is it the more complicated aspects of the English word "feeling." (Sometimes the word "feeling" must be used to translate Thai and Pali words other than *vedanā*.)

*Vijjā.* Knowledge, insight knowledge, wisdom: correct knowledge about the way things really are. Its perfection destroys *avijjā*. Synonymous with *paññā*.

*Vimutti.* Emancipation, deliverance, liberation, release, salvation: becoming free of all attachment, *kilesa*, and *dukkha*, and realizing *nibbāna*.

*Viññāṭa.* Sense-consciousness: knowing sense objects or concerns through the six sense doors (eyes, ears, nose, mouth, body, mind). *Viññāṭa* is the fundamental mental activity required for participation in the sensual world (*loka*); without it there is no experience. Modern Thai uses of *viññāṭa* include "soul" and "spiritual," which, however, are meanings not found in the Pali term. (Compare with *citta* and *mano*.)

*Vipassanā.* Insight: literally, "clear seeing"; to see clearly, distinctly, directly into the true nature of things, into *aniccaṁ*, *dukkhaṁ*, and *anattā*. *Vipassanā* is popularly used to refer to the practice of mental development for the sake of true insight. It is important not to confuse the physical posture, theory, and method of such practices with true realization of impermanence, unsatisfactoriness, and not-self. *Vipassanā* cannot be taught, although methods to nurture it are taught.

*Virāga.* Fading away, dispassion, un-staining: the breaking up, dissolving, and disappearing of *rāga*, of attachment. The lesson of step fourteen.

*Viveka.* Spiritual solitude, aloneness, seclusion: to be undisturbed in quiet solitude and mindfulness. There are three kinds: (1) *kāya-viveka*, physical solitude, when the body is not disturbed; (2) *citta-viveka*, mental solitude, when no defilements disturb the mind; and (3) *upādhi-viveka*, spiritual solitude, freedom from all attachment and all sources of attachment, that is, *nibbāna*.

*Vossagga.* Tossing back, relinquishment: the natural giving away of everything by the liberated mind. Synonymous with *nibbāna* and the same as *paṭinissagga*.

# About the Author

BUDDHADĀSA BHIKKHU (Slave of the Buddha) went forth as a *bhikkhu* (Buddhist monk) in 1926 at the age of twenty. After a few years of study in Bangkok, he was inspired to live close with nature in order to investigate the Buddha-Dhamma as the Buddha had done. Thus, he established Suan Mokkhabalārāma (The Grove of the Power of Liberation) in 1932, near his hometown in Southern Thailand. At that time, it was the only forest Dhamma center in the region, and one of the few places dedicated to *vipassanā* (mental cultivation leading to "seeing clearly" into reality). Word of Buddhadāsa Bhikkhu and Suan Mokkh has spread over the years, and Buddhadāsa Bhikkhu's life and work are considered to be among the most influential events in the Buddhist history of Siam. Here, we can only mention some of the more memorable services he has rendered to Buddhism.

Ajahn Buddhadāsa worked painstakingly to establish and explain the correct and essential principles of pristine Buddhism. That work was based on extensive research of the Pali texts (canon and commentary), especially of the Buddha's Discourses (*sutta-piṭaka*), followed by personal experiment and practice with these teachings. From this, he uncovered the Dhamma that truly quenches *dukkha*, which he in turn shared with anyone interested. His goal was to produce a complete set of references for present and future research and practice. His approach was always scientific, straightforward, and practical.

Although his formal education was limited to seven years, in addition to some beginning Pali studies, during his lifetime he was given seven honorary doctorates by Thai universities. Numerous doctoral theses have been written about his work. His books, both written and transcribed from talks, fill a room at the National Library and influence all serious Thai Buddhists.

Progressive elements in Thai society, especially the young, have been inspired by his wide-ranging thought, teachings, and selfless example. Since the 1960s, activists and thinkers in such areas as education, social welfare, and rural development have drawn upon his teaching, advice, and friendship. His work helped inspire a new generation of socially concerned monks.

He studied all schools of Buddhism and all the major religious traditions. This interest was practical rather than scholarly. He sought to unite all genuinely religious people, meaning those working to overcome selfishness, in order to work together for world peace. This broad-mindedness won him friends and students from around the world, including Christians, Muslims, Hindus, and Sikhs.

Not long before his passing, he established an International Dhamma Hermitage, where courses introducing foreigners to a correct understanding of Buddhist principles and practice are held in English at the beginning of every month. Retreats in Thai are organized for the latter part of each month. Further, he hoped that meetings would be organized for Buddhists from around the world to identify and agree upon the "heart of Buddhism." Finally, he wanted to bring together all the religions to cooperate in helping humanity.

In his last few years, he established some new projects for carrying on the work of serving Lord Buddha and humanity. One is Suan Atammayatārāma, a small training center for foreign monks in a quiet grove near the International Dhamma Hermitage. The guidelines he laid down for this center aim to develop "Dhamma missionaries" who are well versed in the Buddha's teaching, have solid experience of *vipassanā*, and can adapt the Buddha-Dhamma to the problems of the modern world.

Another sister project is Dhamma Mātā (Dhamma Mothers). Society is suffering from a lack of qualified women spiritual teachers; they exist but are not given adequate recognition. Dhamma Mātā aims to raise the status of women by providing them better opportunities and support in Buddhist monastic life and meditation practice. The hope is that there will be more women who can "give birth to others through Dhamma."

Ajahn Buddhadāsa died at Suan Mokkh on 8 July 1993. The work of Suan Mokkh continues as before, according to the law of nature.

# About the Translator

SANTIKARO BHIKKHU (Robert Larson) was born in Chicago and came to Thailand with the Peace Corps in 1980. Ordained in 1985, he came to Suan Mokkh in order to study with Buddhadāsa Bhikkhu. No longer a monk, he now teaches at Liberation Park in rural Wisconsin.

*For further information on the teachings of Buddhadāsa Bhikkhu please contact Suan Mokkh, Ampoe Chaiya, Surat Thani, 84110, Thailand. www.suanmokkh.org*

# Also Available from Wisdom Publications

Heartwood of the Bodhi Tree
*The Buddha's Teachings on Voidness*
Ajahn Buddhadāsa Bhikkhu
Foreword by Donald Swearer and Jack Kornfield

"A remarkable and beautiful book that captures the spacious and profound teachings of the Thai Forest Tradition."
—*Inquiring Mind*

Under the Bodhi Tree
*Buddha's Original Vision of Dependent Co-arising*
Ajahn Buddhadasa Bhikkhu

"A renowned Buddhist master digs into the idea of interdependency—the very core of the Buddha's teachings."

Sons of the Buddha
*The Early Lives of Three Extraordinary Thai Masters*
Kamala Tiyavanich

"Uplifting and, at times, magical"
—*Buddhadharma*

The Four Foundations of Mindfulness
Sayadaw U Sīlānanda
Foreword by Larry Rosenberg

"*The Four Foundations of Mindfulness* is, like all of Wisdom's books, beautiful in all respects."
—Jon Kabat-Zinn, author of *Wherever You Go, There You Are*

How to Meditate
*A Practical Guide*
Kathleen McDonald

"Jewels of wisdom and practical experience to inspire you."
—Richard Gere

Mindfulness, Bliss, and Beyond
*A Meditator's Handbook*
Ajahn Brahm

"Riveting and real. I can't tell you how thrilled I was to read it."
—Glenn Wallis, translator of *The Dhammapada: Verses on the Way*

Pure and Simple
*The Extraordinary Teachings of a Thai Buddhist Laywoman*
Upasika Kee Nanayon
Thanissaro Bhikkhu

"Upasika Kee teaches from her own experience in a voice that is clear and unwavering."
—Sharon Salzberg, author of *Real Happiness*

# About Wisdom Publications

Wisdom Publications is the leading publisher of classic and contemporary Buddhist books and practical works on mindfulness. To learn more about us or to explore our other books, please visit our website at wisdomexperience.org or contact us at the address below.

Wisdom Publications
199 Elm Street
Somerville, MA 02144 USA

We are a 501(c)(3) organization, and donations in support of our mission are tax deductible.

Wisdom Publications is affiliated with the Foundation for the Preservation of the Mahayana Tradition (FPMT).